MASTERING THE SOCIAL STUDIES MEAP TEST: GRADE 5

JAMES KILLORAN

STUART ZIMMER

MARK JARRETT

JARRETT PUBLISHING COMPANY

East Coast:
19 Cross Street
Ronkonkoma, NY 11779
(516) 981-4248

West Coast:
10 Folin Lane
Lafayette, CA 94549
(510) 906-9742

1-800-859-7679 FAX: (516) 588-4722

www.jarrettpub.com

Jarrett Publishing Company
19 Cross Street
Ronkonkoma, New York 11779

ISBN 1-882422-39-2

First Edition
Printed in the United States of America
by Malloy Lithographing, Inc., Ann Arbor, Michigan

10 9 8 7 6 5 4 3 2 1 01 00 99 98

ABOUT THE AUTHORS

James Killoran is a retired Assistant Principal. He has written *Government and You* and *Economics and You*. Mr. Killoran has extensive experience in test writing for the New York State Board of Regents in Social Studies and has served on the Committee for Testing of the National Council of Social Studies. His article on social studies testing has been published in *Social Education*, the country's leading social studies journal. In addition, Mr. Killoran has won a number of awards for outstanding teaching and curriculum development, including, "Outstanding Social Studies Teacher" and "Outstanding Social Studies Supervisor" in New York City. In 1993, he was awarded an Advanced Certificate for Teachers of Social Studies by the N.C.S.S.

Stuart Zimmer is a retired social studies teacher. He has written *Government and You* and *Economics and You*. He served as a test writer for the New York State Board of Regents in social studies and has written for the National Merit Scholarship Examination. In addition, he has published numerous articles on teaching and testing in social studies journals. He has presented many demonstrations and educational workshops at state and national teachers' conferences. In 1989, Mr. Zimmer's achievements were recognized by the New York State Legislature with a Special Legislative Resolution passed in his honor.

Mark Jarrett is a former social studies teacher and a practicing attorney at the San Francisco office of Baker and McKenzie, the world's largest law firm. Mr. Jarrett has served as a test writer for the New York State Board of Regents and has taught at Hofstra University. He was educated at Columbia University, the London School of Economics, the Law School of the University of California at Berkeley, and Stanford University, where he is a doctoral candidate in history. Mr. Jarrett has received several academic awards, including Order of the Coif at Berkeley and the David and Christina Phelps Harris Fellowship at Stanford University.

ALSO BY KILLORAN, ZIMMER AND JARRETT

Michigan: Its Land and Its People
Making Connections: Michigan and the Wider World
The Key to Understanding Global History
The Key to Understanding U.S. History and Government
Mastering Global Studies
Mastering U.S. History and Government
Comprende tu mundo: su historia, sus culturas
Historia y gobierno de los Estados Unidos
Mastering Ohio's 9th Grade Citizenship Test
Mastering Ohio's 12th Grade Citizenship Test
Los Estados Unidos: su historia, su gobierno
Nuestro mundo: su historia, sus culturas
Ohio: Its Land and Its People
Ohio: Its Neighbors, Near and Far
Principios de economía
Texas: Its Land and Its People
New York: Its Land and Its People
North Carolina: The Tar Heel State

ACKNOWLEDGMENTS

The authors would like to thank the following Michigan educators who reviewed the manuscript, and whose comments, suggestions and recommendations proved invaluable:

Michael Yocum
Executive Director, Michigan Council for the Social Studies
Consultant to the Oakland County School District

J. Kelli Sweet
Kalamazoo School District

Cover design by Peter R. Fleck
Layout and typesetting by Maple Hill Press, Ltd., Huntington, NY
Maps and graphics by CF Enterprises

This book is dedicated
...to my wife Donna and my children Christian, Carrie, and Jesse — *James Killoran*
...to my wife Joan and my children Todd and Ronald — *Stuart Zimmer*
...to my wife Goska and my children Alexander and Julia — *Mark Jarrett*

TABLE OF CONTENTS

SECTION 1: LAYING A FOUNDATION

SECTION 2: ANSWERING DIFFERENT TYPES OF QUESTIONS

SECTION 3: REVIEW OF CONTENT STANDARDS, WITH PRACTICE QUESTIONS

SECTION 4: PRACTICE TEST

PHOTO CREDITS

Cover: The Mackinac Bridge, ©1994 Gordon R. Gainer; The Stock Market.

CHAPTER 2:
Page 17: National Archives.

CHAPTER 5:
Page 38: (top) Michigan Travel Bureau; (bottom) Jarrett Archives; Page 40: Holland Visitors and Convention Bureau; Page 41: Michigan State Archives.

CHAPTER 6:
Page 49: (t,m,b) Michigan State Archives; Page 51: Michigan State Archives; Page 52: (t,m,b) Michigan State Archives; Page 53: (t) Ford Motor Company, (b) Vito Palmisano; Page 54: Library of Congress; Page 55: Library of Congress; Page 56: (t) Library of Congress, (b) ©Michigan Bell Telephone Company, 1964; Page 58: Michigan State Archives; Page 59: (t) Library of Congress, (b) N.C. Division of Archives and History; Page 64: (t, l & r) Michigan State Archives, (b,l) Michigan State Archives; (b,r) Ford Motor Company.

CHAPTER 7:
Page 68: (t) Ford Motor Company, (m) Jarrett Archives, (b) Jackson Visitors and Convention Bureau; Page 70: (t) Holland Visitors and Convention Bureau, (b) Lansing Visitors and Convention Bureau; Page 72: Jarrett Archives; Page 78: Jarrett Archives.

CHAPTER 8:
Page 83 (t) Library of Congress, (m) Michigan State Archives, (b) Jarrett Archives; Page 85: Library of Congress; Page 91: Collection of the U.S. Supreme Court.

CHAPTER 10:
Page 106 (t,m,b) Jarrett Archives; Page 108: Library of Congress.

CHAPTER 11:
Page 122: (#1) Holland Visitors and Convention Bureau, (#2) Michigan State Archives; (#3) Ford Motor Company; (#4) Traverse City C.V.B.; (#5) Michigan Travel Bureau; (#6) Mackinaw Area Tourist Bureau; (#7) Jarrett Archives; (#8) Michigan Travel Bureau; Page 142: Jarrett Archives.

CHAPTER 1

WHAT LIES AHEAD

Taking tests is something that all students must do. Everyone wants to do well on the **Social Studies MEAP Test: Grade 5**. Unfortunately, just wanting to do well is not enough. You have to really work at it.

WHAT IS THE MEAP TEST?

The purpose of social studies is to prepare young people to become responsible citizens. In 1996, the Michigan Board of Education approved a new set of content standards in social studies, along with a plan to measure each student's educational development. This plan called for a statewide test in social studies. Knowledge of the content standards will be very important for achieving a good grade on the test.

On the Social Studies MEAP Test, you will be asked questions dealing with several major categories called **strands**:

STRANDS

- geography
- history
- economics
- civics
- inquiry
- public discourse and decision-making

CONTENT STANDARDS

The strands are divided into 22 **content standards**, which spell out what you are expected to know and what you should be able to do by the time you graduate from high school. The social studies content standards are listed on the following chart:

STRANDS / CONTENT STANDARDS

Social Studies Standards for the MEAP Test					
Historical Perspective	***Geographic Perspective***	***Civic Perspective***	***Economic Perspective***	***Inquiry***	***Public Discourse and Decision-Making***
I.1 *Time and Chronology*	**II.1** *People, Places and Cultures*	**III.1** *Purposes of Government*	**IV.1** *Individual and Household Choices*	**V.1** *Information Processing*	**VI.1** *Identifying and Analyzing Issues*
I.2 *Comprehending the Past*	**II.2** *Human/ Environment Interaction*	**III.2** *Ideals of American Democracy*	**IV.2** *Business Choices*		**VI.2** *Persuasive Writing*
I.3 *Analyzing and Interpreting the Past*	**II.3** *Location, Movement and Connections*	**III.3** *Democracy in Action*	**IV.3** *Role of Government*		
I.4 *Judging Decisions from the Past*	**II.4** *Regions, Patterns and Processes*	**III.4** *American Government and Politics*	**IV.4** *Economic Systems*		
	II.5 *Global Issues and Events*	**III.5** *American Government and World Affairs*	**IV.5** *Trade*		

THE "BIG IDEAS" AND THEIR BENCHMARKS

Each of the content standards contains a "big idea." Each "big idea" has a list of benchmarks that explain specifically what you should know and what you should be able to do at various grade levels. The benchmarks are used to trace your progress at different times during your educational career.

For example, let's look at the fifth-grade benchmarks for the first content standard under the first strand: *Historical Perpective.*

Strand: Historical Perspective

Content Standard I.1: Time and Chronology

All students will sequence events in time in order to examine relationships among them to explain cause and effect.

Benchmarks. By fifth grade, students will:
- Measure chronological time by decades and centuries.
- Place major events in the development of their local community and the state of Michigan in chronological order.
- Place major events in the history of the United States in chronological order.

The *content standards* give a general description of the "big ideas" in each strand. You will then be tested on your ability to do the specific things outlined in the *benchmarks*. For example, the second benchmark (shown on the card above) requires that you know how to put the major events of Michigan's history into chronological order. This means you must have a general idea of when these major events occurred. At the end of each review chapter in this book is a listing of the benchmarks for the strand covered in that chapter.

THE TEST FORMAT

There are three types of questions on the fifth grade Social Studies MEAP Test. They all follow the same pattern.

The questions require you to know and understand the material listed in the benchmarks. You must also be able to apply this knowledge to a "prompt." A **prompt** is information presented in the question in the form of a reading, map, chart, graph, drawing, or other material. The prompt is used to activate your *prior knowledge* (what you already know in social studies).

Thus, to do well on this test you have to understand both:

- ✦ how to analyze different types of prompts, and
- ✦ what you must know and do, according to the benchmarks.

HOW THIS BOOK IS ORGANIZED

You will be responsible for knowledge you have learned from kindergarten through the fifth grade. How can you be expected to remember so much information? With this book as your guide, you should find the test much less difficult — and maybe even fun to study for. ***Mastering The Social Studies MEAP Test: Grade 5*** will help you prepare to answer any type of question found on the test.

The following section-by-section review tells you what you will find in this book.

SECTION 1: WHAT LIES AHEAD

The opening chapter, which you are reading, introduces you to the Social Studies MEAP Test for the fifth grade. It also describes how this book is organized.

SECTION 2: ANSWERING DIFFERENT TYPES OF QUESTIONS

This section of the book consists of three chapters. They focus on two of the three types of questions that appear on the MEAP Test. The third type of question, the extended-response question, is covered in Chapter 10.

- ✦ **Chapter 2** deals with prompts. On the MEAP Test, each type of question begins with a prompt which you must be able to interpret.

- ✦ **Chapter 3** focuses on how to answer selected-response questions. In these questions, you will be asked to "select" the correct answer from a group of four possible choices.

- ✦ **Chapter 4** examines how to answer constructed-response questions. In these questions, you will be asked to do a short task such as filling in a chart, writing a paragraph, or completing a map.

SECTION 3: REVIEW OF THE CONTENT STRANDS

This section provides brief summaries of the information you need to review for the five strands on the Social Studies MEAP Test. Each chapter contains a brief or capsule summary of the basic information you need to know for that strand. Each chapter also has a summary of the strand's "big ideas." It is followed by a series of practice questions. The chapter ends with a listing of that strand's benchmarks.

- ✦ **Chapter 5** reviews **geography**. It focuses on the physical and cultural geography of Michigan and the main regions of the United States.

- **Chapter 6** reviews **history**. It summarizes the history of Michigan and the history of the United States until 1763.

- **Chapter 7** reviews **economics**. It emphasizes the major terms and concepts of economics and explains the workings of the free market system.

- **Chapter 8** reviews **civics**. It describes the American system of democratic government, including the role and structure of federal and state government.

- **Chapter 9** reviews **inquiry**. This chapter explains how to answer constructed-response questions on the inquiry section of the test.

- **Chapter 10** reviews **public discourse and decision-making**, including the "core democratic values." The chapter concludes with a section on how to answer an extended-response question on a public policy issue. The sample question is similar to the extended-response questions on the Social Studies MEAP Test: Grade 5.

SECTION 3: A PRACTICE TEST

The final section of this book contains **Chapter 11**, a complete practice Social Studies MEAP Test. You should take this practice test under conditions similar to those of the actual test. This practice test will allow you to spot areas of weakness that need further review, and will increase your confidence. You can go over the answers with your teacher in class as a final review before taking the real MEAP Test.

By paying careful attention to your teachers at school, by completing your homework assignments, and by preparing with this book, you can be confident that you will do your best when the day of the real MEAP Test arrives.

CHAPTER 2

DIFFERENT TYPES OF PROMPTS

On the Social Studies MEAP Test: Grade 5, there will be three types of questions:

- ✦ Selected-Response Questions
- ✦ Constructed-Response Questions
- ✦ Extended-Response Questions

Each of these types of questions will test your knowledge of Michigan's social studies curriculum. The questions will ask you to apply your prior knowledge of social studies to a **prompt** *(a piece of data)*.

Each of the questions assumes that you know how to interpret the various prompts. You cannot begin to answer the questions until you **understand the prompt.** In this chapter, you will examine the major types of prompts found on the test:

- Maps
- Bar Graphs
- Line Graphs
- Pie Charts
- Tables
- Timelines
- Drawings and Photographs
- Reading Selections

Our discussion of each prompt will be divided into three parts:

1. A description of the type of prompt.

2. An examination of each part of the prompt, to help you interpret it.

3. Comprehension questions to check your understanding. (These questions will only test your ability to *interpret* prompts. They are not the same as MEAP Test questions, which are found throughout the rest of this book.)

MAPS

WHAT IS A MAP?

A map is a drawing of a geographic area. There are many kinds of maps. Some of the most common are:

- **Political maps**, showing the major boundaries between countries or states.
- **Physical maps**, showing the physical characteristics of a region, such as rivers, mountains, vegetation and elevation *(height above sea level)*.
- **Product maps**, providing information on the natural resources and agricultural and industrial products of an area.
- **Theme maps**, providing information on a theme such as rainfall, languages spoken, average temperatures or main points of interest.

STEPS TO UNDERSTANDING A MAP

1. Look at the Title. The title of the map tells you what kind of information is presented. For example, the title of the map below indicates that it shows the annual (yearly) amount of rainfall in various parts of Michigan.

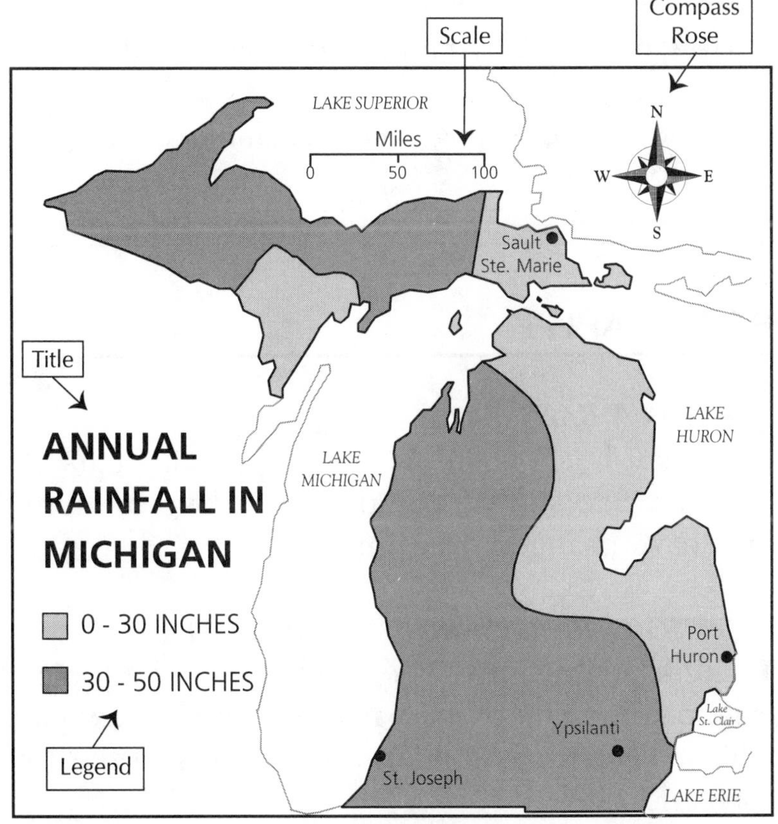

2. Look at the Legend. The legend, or **key**, lists the symbols used and identifies what they represent. In this map:

- the light gray areas have 0 to 30 inches of rain a year.
- the dark gray areas have 30 to 50 inches of rain a year.

3. Look at the Compass Rose. It shows the four basic directions: north, south, east, and west. If there is no compass rose, you can usually assume that north is at the top and south is at the bottom.

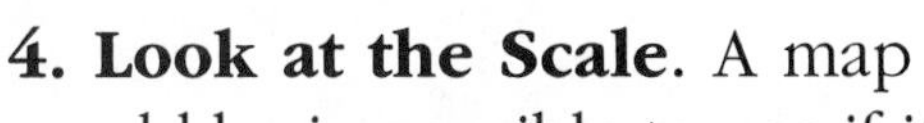

4. Look at the Scale. A map would be impossible to use if it were the same size as the area it shows. Mapmakers reduce the size so that it can fit onto a page. The scale is used to indicate the real distance between places on the map. The distance is usually shown in miles (or kilometers). For example, on one map an inch may represent 1 mile, while on another map an inch may represent 100 miles.

Finding Specific Information. To find specific information, you must use the legend and other map features together. For example, if you wanted to find which part of the Lower Peninsula gets the most annual rainfall, here is what you must do:

1. Find the Lower Peninsula on the map on page 7. Notice that part of it is shown in light gray, and part of it is shown in dark gray.
2. Look at the legend for the meaning of the light and dark gray shadings.
3. Since the eastern part of the Lower Peninsula is shown in light gray, it gets between 20 and 30 inches of rainfall a year. The western part, shown in dark gray, gets between 30 and 50 inches of rainfall a year. Thus, the western part of the Lower Peninsula gets the most annual rainfall.

INTERPRETING A MAP

Now answer the following questions, using the map on page 7.

CHECKING YOUR UNDERSTANDING

How much yearly rainfall does most of the Upper Peninsula get? ____________

If you were traveling from Ypsilanti to Sault Ste. Marie, in which direction would you be going? ______________________________________

BAR GRAPHS

WHAT IS A BAR GRAPH?

A bar graph is a chart made up of parallel bars of different lengths. A bar graph is often used to show a comparison of two or more things. Sometimes it shows how they have changed over time.

STEPS TO UNDERSTANDING A BAR GRAPH

1. Look at the Title. The title tells you the topic of the information presented. For example, the title of the bar graph on the next page indicates that the graph shows which regions of the world immigrants to the United States came from, between 1900 and 1995.

Name______________________ Teacher______________________

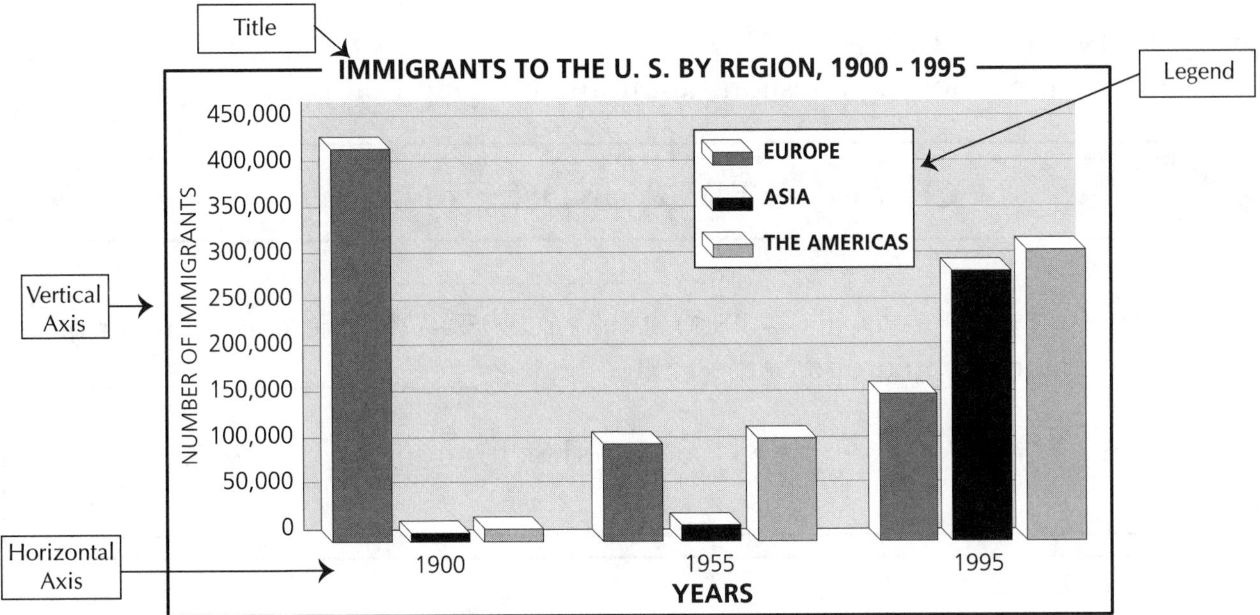

2. Look at the Legend. It shows what each bar represents. In the graph above:

- the dark gray bars represent Europe
- the black bars represent Asia
- the light gray bars represent the Americas (North and South America)

3. Look at the Vertical and the Horizontal Axis.

- The **vertical axis** runs from top to bottom. It usually measures the length of the bars. Here, it lists the number of immigrants — from 0 to 450,000.

- The **horizontal axis** runs from left to right. It usually identifies the bars. Here the horizontal axis indicates the years being compared: 1900, 1955 and 1995.

> **Note:** Some bar graphs show bars running sideways instead of up and down. The only difference between an up-and-down bar graph and a sideways one is that the axes are reversed.

Finding Specific Information. To find specific information, you must examine the features of the bar graph closely. For example, to find out how many immigrants came to the United States from Europe in 1900, here is what to do:

1. On the horizontal axis, find the year 1900.
2. Choose the bar that represents Europe. According to the legend, this is the dark gray bar.
3. Run your finger to the top of the bar, and slide it slightly to the left. When you reach the vertical axis, you will find it is between 400,000 and 450,000. This shows that the number of immigrants from Europe in 1900 was about 425,000.

Interpreting a Bar Graph

Now answer the following questions about the bar graph on page 9.

CHECKING YOUR UNDERSTANDING

In which of the three years — 1900, 1955 or 1995 — did the least number of people come from Europe to the United States? ____________________

How many immigrants came to the United States from Asia in 1955?

____

LINE GRAPHS

What Is a Line Graph?

A line graph is a chart composed of a series of points connected by a line. A line graph is often used to show how something has changed over a period of time.

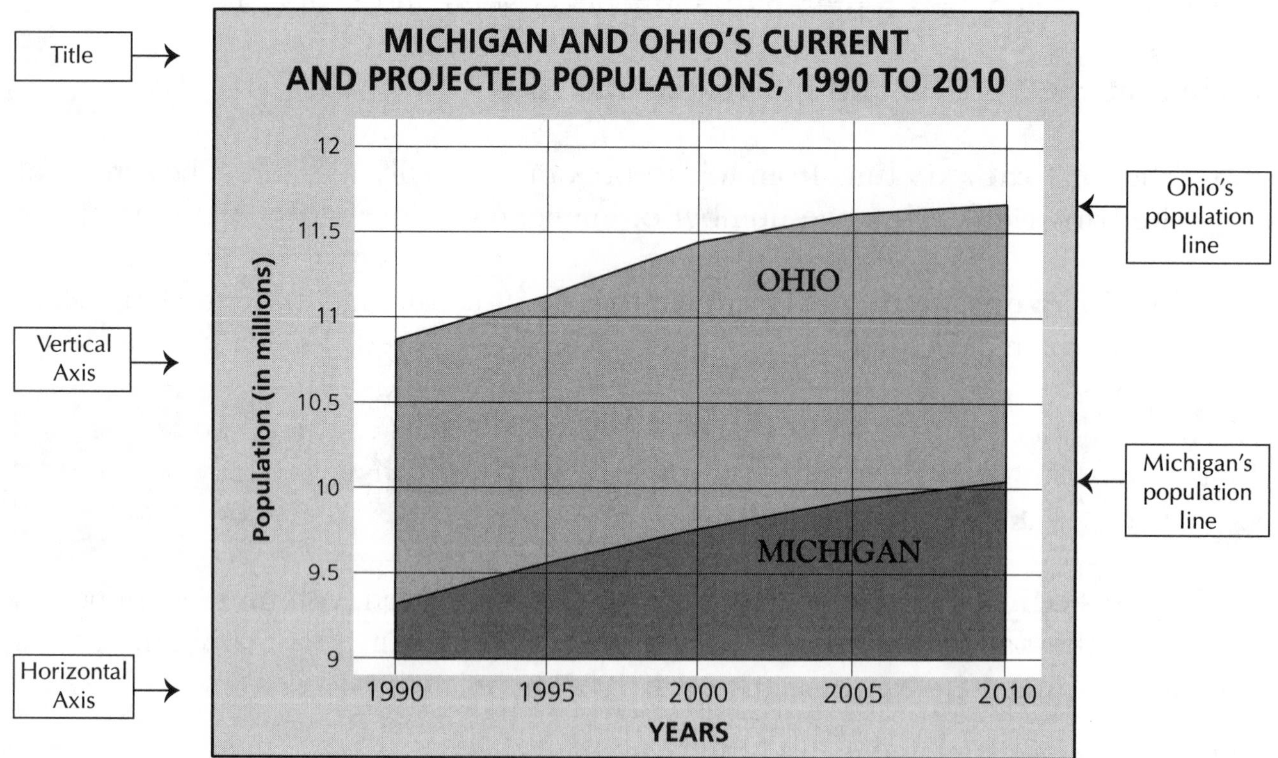

Steps to Understanding a Line Graph

1. Look at the Title. The title tells you the topic of the graph. In the example above, the title indicates that this line graph compares the populations of two states, Michigan and Ohio, in the recent past and into the future.

Name______________________ Teacher______________________

2. Look at the Vertical Axis and the Horizontal Axis.

- The **vertical axis** runs from bottom to top. It often measures the size of something. As you move up the vertical axis, the numbers get larger. Note that the vertical axis in this line graph is showing the population in millions: the number 9 represents 9 million people.

- The **horizontal axis** runs from left to right. In this line graph, the horizontal axis shows years. The first year is 1990, and the dates continue in five-year intervals until 2010.

3. Look at the Legend. If there is a legend, it explains what each line represents. If a graph has only one or two lines, there is often no legend because the information is marked directly on the graph. If a graph has many lines, however, a legend is often needed. In this graph, the **top** line indicates **Ohio's population**, while the **lower** line shows **Michigan's population**.

Finding Specific Information. For specific information, you must examine the two axes. For example, what is Michigan's projected population for the year 2010?

- First, run your finger across the horizontal axis until you reach the year 2010.

- Now move your finger up until you reach the line representing Michigan. To find the actual number, slide your finger to the left until you reach the numbers on the vertical axis. This point intersects just above the "10" line.

- Thus, Michigan's population in the year 2010 is projected to be about 10,000,000 people.

INTERPRETING A LINE GRAPH

Now answer the following questions about the line graph on the previous page.

CHECKING YOUR UNDERSTANDING

What was the difference in population between Ohio and Michigan in 1990?

____

What is Michigan's population projected to be in the year 2000?

____

Name______________________ Teacher______________________

PIE CHARTS

What Is a Pie Chart?

A pie chart, also called a circle graph, is a circle divided into sections of different sizes. A pie chart is often used to show relationships between a whole and its parts.

Steps to Understanding a Pie Chart

1. Look at the Title. The title tells you the overall topic. For example, this pie chart shows which groups own parts of Michigan's forest land.

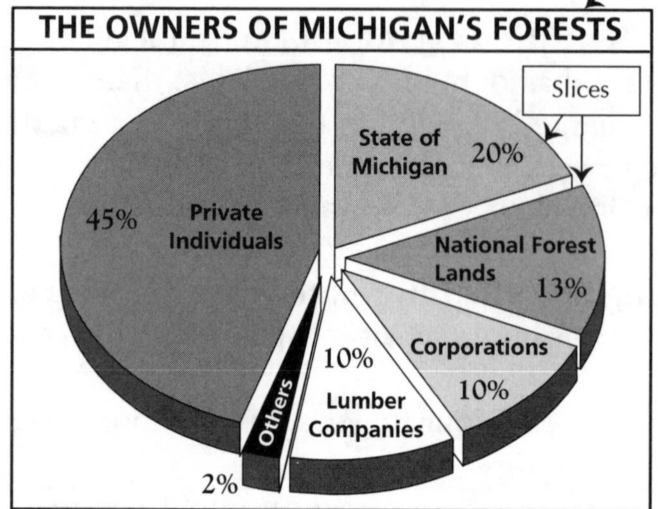

2. Look at the Slices. Each slice shows its size or relationship to the whole pie. Think of the pie as 100% of something. If you add all the slices together, they will total 100%. In this pie, there are six different groups that own parts of Michigan's forests. These groups are named on the pie slices.

3. Look at the Legend. Sometimes a pie chart has a legend showing what each slice of the pie represents. In many pie charts, a legend is not needed. Instead, the information is shown on the slices, as in the pie chart above.

Finding Specific Information

To find specific information, you have to examine each slice. For example, if you want to know the percentage of Michigan forest land owned by lumber companies, find the slice marked "Lumber Companies." It is labeled 10% of the total.

Interpreting a Pie Chart

Now answer the following questions about the pie chart above.

CHECKING YOUR UNDERSTANDING

Which owns more of Michigan's forest land — the national government or the state of Michigan? ______________________________

What percentage of Michigan's forest land is controlled by corporations other than lumber companies? ______________________________

Name______________________________ Teacher______________________________

TABLES

WHAT IS A TABLE?

A table is an arrangement of words or numbers in columns and rows. A table is often used to organize large amounts of information so individual facts can be easily located and compared.

Title

Column Headings (Categories)

NUMBER, ACREAGE AND FARMLAND OF MICHIGAN FARMS, 1960-1994

Year	Number of Farms	Average Farm Size	Total Farmland in Acres
1994	52,000	206 acres	10,700,000
1990	54,000	200 acres	10,800,000
1980	65,000	175 acres	11,400,000
1970	84,000	151 acres	12,700,000
1960	118,000	131 acres	15,400,000

Rows

STEPS TO UNDERSTANDING A TABLE

1. Look at the Title. The title states the overall topic. For example, the table above provides information about the number of Michigan farms, the average size of each farm and the total amount of Michigan farmland, during selected years — starting in 1960 and ending in 1994.

2. Look at the Categories. Each table has various categories of information. These categories are named in the **column headings** across the top of the table. In this table, there are four different categories: *Year, Number of Farms, Average Farm Size,* and *Total Farmland in Acres*. The **rows** contain information for each category.

Finding Specific Information

For specific information, you must find where the **columns** and **rows** intersect. For example, if you wanted to know the total number of acres of Michigan's farmland in 1960, here is what to do:

- Put your right index finger on the column marked *Total Farmland in Acres.* This column shows Michigan's farmland in acres for various years.
- Put your left index finger on the column marked *Year*. Slide your finger down until it reaches the row for the year *"1960."*
- Slide your right finger down the *Total Farmland* column to the *"1960"* row.

- You can see that the total of Michigan's farmland in 1960 was 15,400,000 acres.

INTERPRETING A TABLE

Now answer the following questions about the table on the previous page.

CHECKING YOUR UNDERSTANDING

What was the average size of a Michigan farm in 1970? ________________

What were the total acres of Michigan farmland in 1980? ________________

TIMELINES

WHAT IS A TIMELINE?

A timeline shows a group of events arranged in chronological order along a line. **Chronological order** is the order in which these events occurred. The first event to occur is the first event that appears on the timeline. A timeline can span anything from a short period to several thousand years. The main function of a timeline is to show how events are related to each other. Timelines can be made horizontally or vertically. You may see them either way on the MEAP Test.

Title → **KEY EVENTS IN MICHIGAN'S AUTO INDUSTRY**

Dates →	1896	1899	1902	1903	1908	1914	1925
Events →	Ransom E. Olds introduces 4-wheeled gas-powered auto	Olds Motor Works builds nation's first auto factory in Detroit	Cadillac Motor Company is organized	Ford Motor Company is founded in Detroit	William Durant founds General Motors; Ford begins selling Model T's	Henry Ford announces $5 daily wage and 8-hour workday	Chrysler Motors is organized

STEPS TO UNDERSTANDING A TIMELINE

1. Look at the Title. The title tells you the general topic of the timeline. For example, in the sample above the title indicates that the timeline lists important events or "milestones" in making Michigan the nation's leading producer of automobiles.

Name________________________ Teacher________________________

2. Look at the Events. Events on the timeline are related to the title. For example, in this timeline each event was a major achievement of Michigan's auto industry.

3. Look at the Dates. Events are placed on the timeline in chronological order according to their date. A timeline is always based on a particular time period, no matter how brief or long. For example, this timeline starts at the end of the 19th century and continues until the early 20th century.

If you add another event, its date might fall between two dates on the timeline. For example, if you wanted to add that in 1909 Michigan built the first mile of concrete highway in the country, where on the timeline would that event go? Since 1909 is closer to 1908 *(1 year)* than it is to 1914 *(5 years)*, you would place it on the timeline closer to 1908 than to 1914.

4. Be Aware of Special Terms. To understand questions about timelines or time periods, you should be familiar with two special terms:

- ✦ A **decade** is a ten-year period.
- ✦ A **century** is a 100-year period.

Note. Identifying centuries may seem confusing at first. For example, the 20th century refers to the 100 years from 1901 to 2000. This numbering system came about because we start counting from the year it is believed that Christ was born. Thus, the first one hundred years after the birth of Christ were the years 1-100. This is called the **first century**. The second century went from 101-200; the third century was from 201 to 300, and so on.

5. Look at the Passage of Time. Remember that events are arranged from the earliest event (on the left) to the most recent event (on the right). To measure the number of years from one date to another, subtract the smaller date from the larger date. If it is the year 1999, how long has it been since Michigan was admitted as a state in 1837? By subtracting 1837 from 1999, we find that it was 262 years ago:

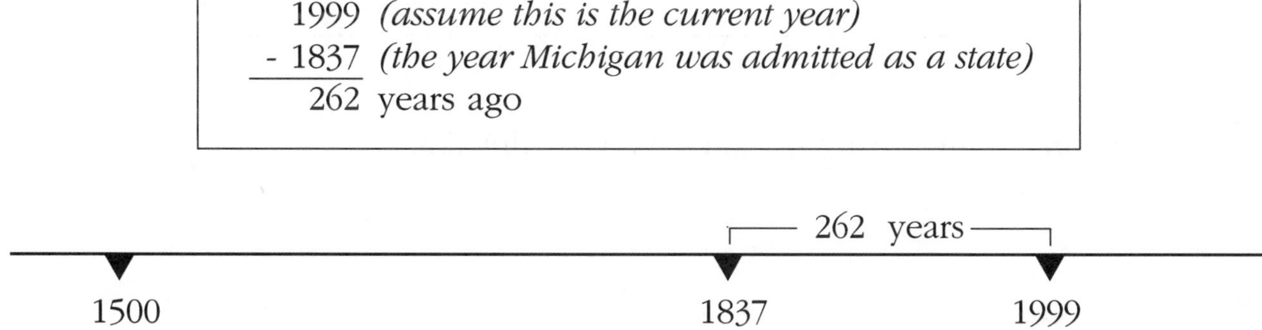

Interpreting a Timeline

Now that you have read about timelines, answer the following questions about the timeline on page 14.

CHECKING YOUR UNDERSTANDING

Which century includes the years 1801-1900? ____________________

What will the next century, 2001-2100, be called? ____________________

On what industry does the timeline focus? ____________________

How many decades are covered by the timeline? ____________________

Which event happened first: the founding of General Motors or the organization of the Cadillac Motor Company?

____

Creating a Timeline

Let's put your understanding of timelines to work. Below is a list of events and when they occurred. Use this information to create a timeline.

1985: Michigan's mandatory seat-belt law goes into effect
1974: Gerald Ford is the first Michigander to become President
1977: Detroit's Renaissance Center is completed
1990: John Engler is elected Governor of Michigan
1984: Detroit Tigers win the Baseball World Series
1995: General Motors and Ford report record earnings

Use the graphic on the next page to create your timeline:

Name ____________________ Teacher ____________________

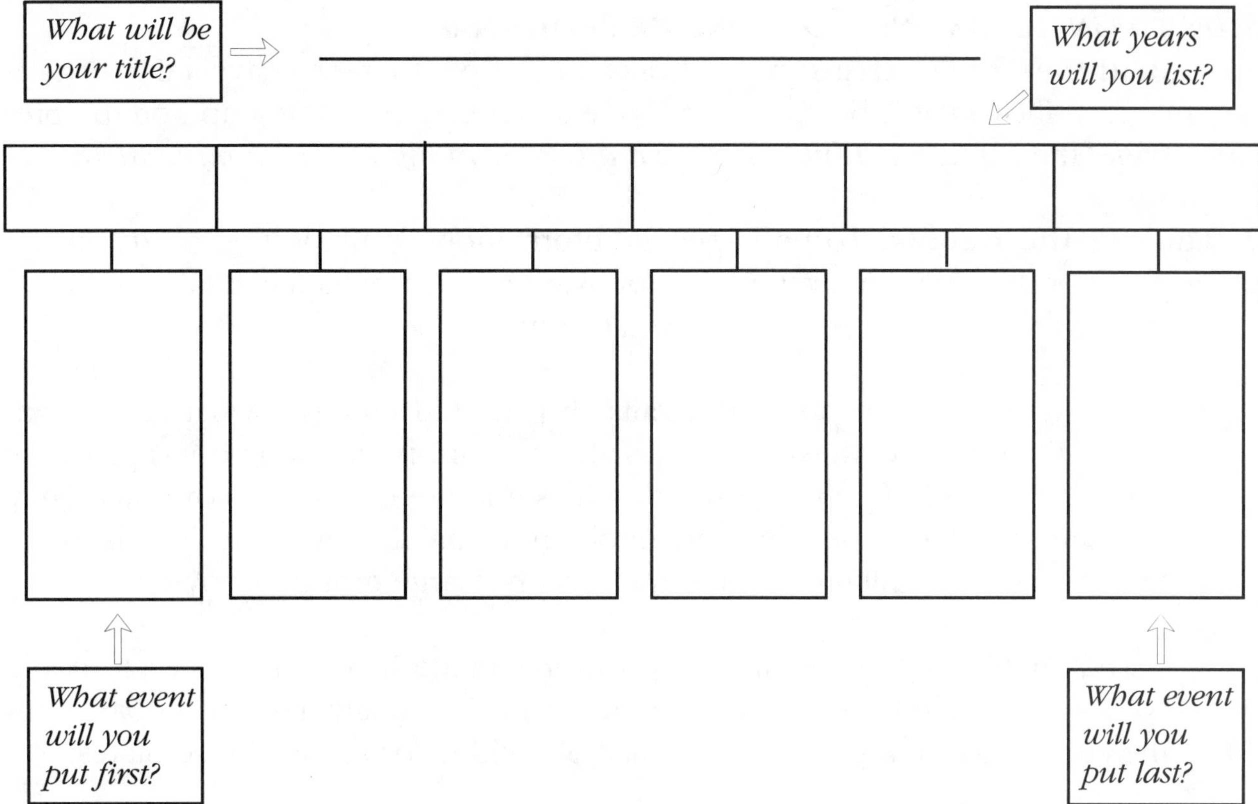

DRAWINGS AND PHOTOGRAPHS

What Is a Drawing or Photograph?

A drawing or photograph shows how something looked in the past or looks today. Drawings and photographs are especially useful for understanding the past by showing how people looked and dressed, and what they once did. Often, a photograph allows us to get the "feeling" of an earlier period of time or a different place. Since photography was not invented until the mid-1800s, we rely on artists' drawings and paintings to show what things looked like before that time.

Children after a day of working in a coal mine in 1870.

Name______________________________ Teacher______________________________

Steps to Understanding a Drawing or Photograph

1. Look at the Title or Caption. Most drawings or photographs have a title or caption that identifies what is being shown. For example, in the photograph on the previous page, the caption is *Children after a day of working in a coal mine in 1870.*

2. Look at the Details. To find specific information, examine the *details* in the photograph or drawing. For example, if you want to know what child labor was like for some children in the 1870s, here is what to do:

- Carefully look at the physical details shown, and consider what they might mean. For example, this photograph shows a group of young boys, probably age 10 to 12. All of them are wearing hats and are dressed in coveralls. They have heavy gloves. Their faces are dirty. They don't look very healthy. None of the children are smiling — unusual for such a large group of boys.

- Based on this photograph, it seems clear that in the 1870s one group of people who worked in coal mines were young boys. Eventually, laws were passed in the early 1900s that prevented the use of child labor in the United States.

Interpreting a Drawing or Photograph

Now that you have looked over the photograph, answer the following questions.

CHECKING YOUR UNDERSTANDING

Do you think these boys enjoyed their work? ____________________

Explain. ____

Do you think these children attended school? ____________________

Explain. ____

What jobs do you think these boys did in the mine? ____________________

____

Name____________________ Teacher____________________

READING SELECTIONS

WHAT IS A READING SELECTION?

A reading selection consists of a statement or a group of statements about a particular topic or subject. It may be a brief quotation or a short paragraph. The main function of the selection is to present someone's ideas about a topic.

STEPS TO UNDERSTANDING A READING SELECTION

To better understand a reading selection you should note that the writer presents a series of facts to prove a point. Ask yourself the following questions about each reading selection:

- What do you know about the writer?
- What term, concept or situation is being discussed by the writer?
- What is the writer saying about the term, concept or situation?
- What facts does the writer present to support his or her views?
- What is the main idea of the reading selection?

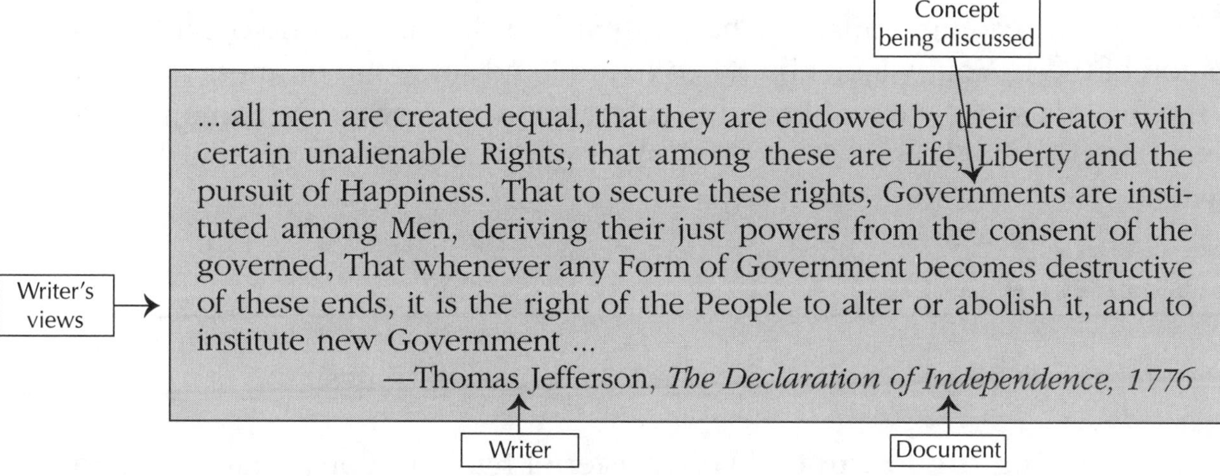

Concept being discussed
Writer's views
... all men are created equal, that they are endowed by their Creator with certain unalienable Rights, that among these are Life, Liberty and the pursuit of Happiness. That to secure these rights, Governments are instituted among Men, deriving their just powers from the consent of the governed, That whenever any Form of Government becomes destructive of these ends, it is the right of the People to alter or abolish it, and to institute new Government ...
—Thomas Jefferson, The Declaration of Independence, 1776
Writer
Document

INTERPRETING A READING SELECTION

Now answer the following questions about the reading selection above.

CHECKING YOUR UNDERSTANDING

What is the main idea of the selection? ______________________________

____

Why were the words in this reading passage important to the future of the United States? ______________________________

____

Name______________________ Teacher______________________

CHAPTER 3

ANSWERING SELECTED-RESPONSE QUESTIONS

There will be three types of questions on the MEAP Test: selected, constructed, and extended response. In this chapter you will examine **selected-response** questions.

THE STRUCTURE OF THE QUESTION

Selected-response questions consist of a prompt followed by a cluster of five multiple-choice questions. The prompt on which these questions are based will vary. It could be a short reading, a map, a chart, a graph, a drawing, a photograph or a combination of these. You will first be asked to read and study the prompt. Then for each of the five questions, you will need to select the best answer from among four possible choices. You will have to use both the prompt and your prior social studies knowledge to choose the right answer.

WHAT'S BEING ASKED?

In selected-response questions you are being tested on **two** things:

- **Understanding the Prompts.** Every cluster of five questions centers around a prompt or prompts. It is assumed that you know how to read and analyze the prompt. (Chapter 2 has already focused on interpreting various prompts.)

- **Understanding the Benchmarks.** It is not enough to just interpret the various prompts, because test questions will ask you to go one step further. You will also need to use your prior knowledge to choose the correct answer. This prior knowledge is based on your mastery of the benchmarks, which outline Michigan's curriculum for fifth grade social studies.

REMEMBER: You will **NOT** be able to answer the questions just from your understanding of the prompt. You must also apply your knowledge of the social studies **benchmarks**.

Let's look at an example of a cluster of questions that could be used to test your understanding of the ***Geographic Perspective*** strand.

SAMPLE CLUSTER OF GEOGRAPHY QUESTIONS

Directions: Study the following map and use it with what you already know to answer the questions that follow.

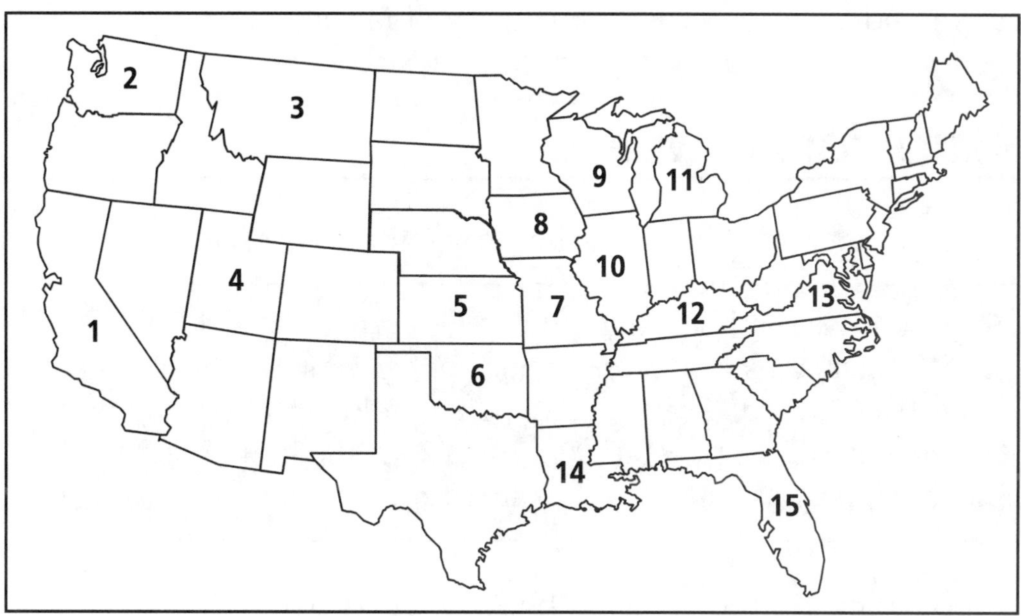

1 Which pair of states is MOST influenced by trade with Asia?

A States 1 and 2
B States 13 and 15
C States 14 and 15
D States 9 and 11

2 Which geographic feature is shared by State 7 and State 10?

A Both states border the Everglades.
B The Rocky Mountains run through both states.
C Both states border the Mississippi River.
D One of the Great Lakes touches both states.

3 Which of the following BEST explains the similarities between the economic activities of State 5 and State 8?

A Both have large areas suitable for farming.
B Both are located on the Great Lakes.
C Both have large oil deposits.
D Both are located on the Mississippi River.

Name ______________________ Teacher ______________________

4 Which state would MOST likely be a center for the fishing industry?

A State 14
B State 3
C State 12
D State 4

5 Based on the information in the map, which statement is accurate?

A State 9 and State 11 border the Great Lakes.
B More states border the Pacific Ocean than the Atlantic Ocean.
C State 14 and State 15 border the country of Mexico.
D State 1 and State 14 border the Gulf of Mexico.

EXPLANATION OF ANSWERS

1 Which pair of states is MOST influenced by trade with Asia?

The answer is **A**. The benchmark being tested here is to "locate and describe major places, cultures, and communities of the United States." Using the map and your background knowledge , you should realize that the west coast of the United States faces the continent of Asia. Of the four choices, *only* California and Washington (States 1 and 2) are located on the west coast. **[II.1.LE.3]**

2 Which geographic feature is shared by State 7 and State 10?

The answer is **C**. The benchmark being tested here is to "describe the geography of major U.S. regions." Using the map and your background knowledge of the major physical features of the United States, you should realize that, of the four choices, only Illinois and Missouri (States 10 and 7) both border a major river — the Mississippi River. **[II.4.LE.6]**

3 Which of the following BEST explains the similarities between the economic activities of State 5 and State 8?

The answer is **A**. The benchmark being tested here is to "describe the major physical ecosystems, resources and land uses of the state, region, and the country." Using the map and your background knowledge of major land uses of the United States, you should know that both Kansas (State 5) and Iowa (State 8) are located in the great wheat and corn growing region of the central United States. **[II.2.LE.3]**

Name ______________________________ Teacher ______________________________

4 Which state would MOST likely be a center for the fishing industry?

> The answer is **A**. The benchmark being tested here is to "describe and explain major kinds of economic activity." Using the map and your background knowledge of major U.S. water systems, you should realize that of the four choices, only Louisiana (State 14) is located on a large body of water, the Gulf of Mexico, which would be necessary to support a fishing industry. **[II.3.LE.1]**

5 Based on the information in the map, which statement is accurate?

> The answer is **A**. The benchmark being tested here deals with the Great Lakes ecosystem. Using the map and your background knowledge of the location of the Great Lakes, you should realize that Michigan (State 11) and Wisconsin (State 9) border the Great Lakes. The other three statements are inaccurate. **[II.4.LE.5]**

SUMMARY

Since clusters of five questions will make up the majority of the test, it is worthwhile to review the two major keys for answering them.

- ✦ **KEY #1.** Every cluster of questions will center around a prompt or a series of prompts. Each question assumes that you know how to read, analyze, and understand the overall meaning of the prompt. Chapter 2 focused on interpreting prompts. Make sure you know how to "read" the various types of prompts.

- ✦ **KEY #2.** You **CANNOT** get the correct answer just by understanding the prompt. The prompt is used as a means for you to apply your prior knowledge to the information shown in the prompt. The required knowledge you will need to apply is outlined in the **benchmarks**. The benchmarks for each content standard are listed on the last page of each content chapter.

CHAPTER 4

ANSWERING CONSTRUCTED-RESPONSE QUESTIONS

Unlike selected-response questions, in which you select an answer from a list of four choices, **constructed-response questions** require you to create your own answer to a question or a series of questions. Like selected-response questions, this type of question tests your understanding of the"big ideas" found in the benchmarks. There are five constructed-response questions on the 5th grade Social Studies MEAP Test — one for each strand: geography, history, economics, civics, and inquiry.

THE "ACTION WORDS"

Many constructed-response questions will ask you to write something. What they specifically ask you to write will be stated in the "**action words**" of the question. Following are some of the most common action words and hints on how to respond to them.

✦IDENTIFY

Identify means to "name something." It is generally used when you name one or more causes, features, or changes. For example,

- **Sample Question:** *Identify* a major ecosystem of the United States.
- **Hint:** To identify something is to **name it**. You do not have to describe or explain it — simply name it.
- **Answer:** Here is one model answer to the sample question above:

A major ecosystem of the United States is the Great Lakes ecosystem.

✦ DESCRIBE

Describe means to **tell about** something.

- **Sample Question**: *Describe* the Great Lakes.

- **Hints:** To describe something is usually to tell about the *what, who, when,* and *where.* Start by answering the *what* first. Try to draw a word picture of what you are describing. Then answer the *who, when* and *where* if they apply.

- **Answer:** Here is one model answer to the sample question above:

> *The Great Lakes are five large lakes in the Midwestern United States and Canada. They stretch from Wisconsin to New York. The Great Lakes are among the largest freshwater lakes in the world. They hold one-fifth of the world's fresh water.*

✦ EXPLAIN, GIVE, OR PROVIDE

Explain, give, or provide means to give the reasons or causes of something.

- **Sample Question**: *Explain* why fruits are grown in the Lower Peninsula.

- **Hints**: When explaining something, **provide facts** that support your position. An *explain, give* or *provide* question asks for the *why* of something. Start by stating what you have to explain. Then give reasons that support your statement.

- **Answer**: Here is one model answer to the sample question above:

> *There are several reasons why fruits are grown in the Lower Peninsula. The Lower Peninsula has adequate rainfall and fertile soil. The growing season is long enough for fruits to grow. The land is flat, so fruits are easy to plant and harvest with farm machines. The Lower Peninsula also has a good highway system connecting its farms to cities. These highways allow farmers to send their fresh fruits to markets where they can be sold.*

✦ SHOW

Show means to point out how something works or how it came about.

- **Sample Question**: *Show* how the Great Lakes affect Michigan's climate.

- **Hints**: To show something is usually to present the **how** of something. It is different from "explain" in that you are not asked to present a series of reasons to prove a point. Instead, you are asked to present the parts that make up the whole. Answering a *show* question is like painting a picture that displays different parts.

- **Answer:** Here is one model answer to the sample question above:

> *The Great Lakes have an important effect on Michigan's climate. Water changes its temperature less quickly than land. The Great Lakes warm the winds passing over them during the winter months. These winds then warm parts of the state. In summer, the Great Lakes are cooler than the surrounding land. Winds passing across the lakes help cool the state.*

A SAMPLE QUESTION

Directions: You should take about 5 minutes to study the map and read the question. Use it with what you already know to complete the task.

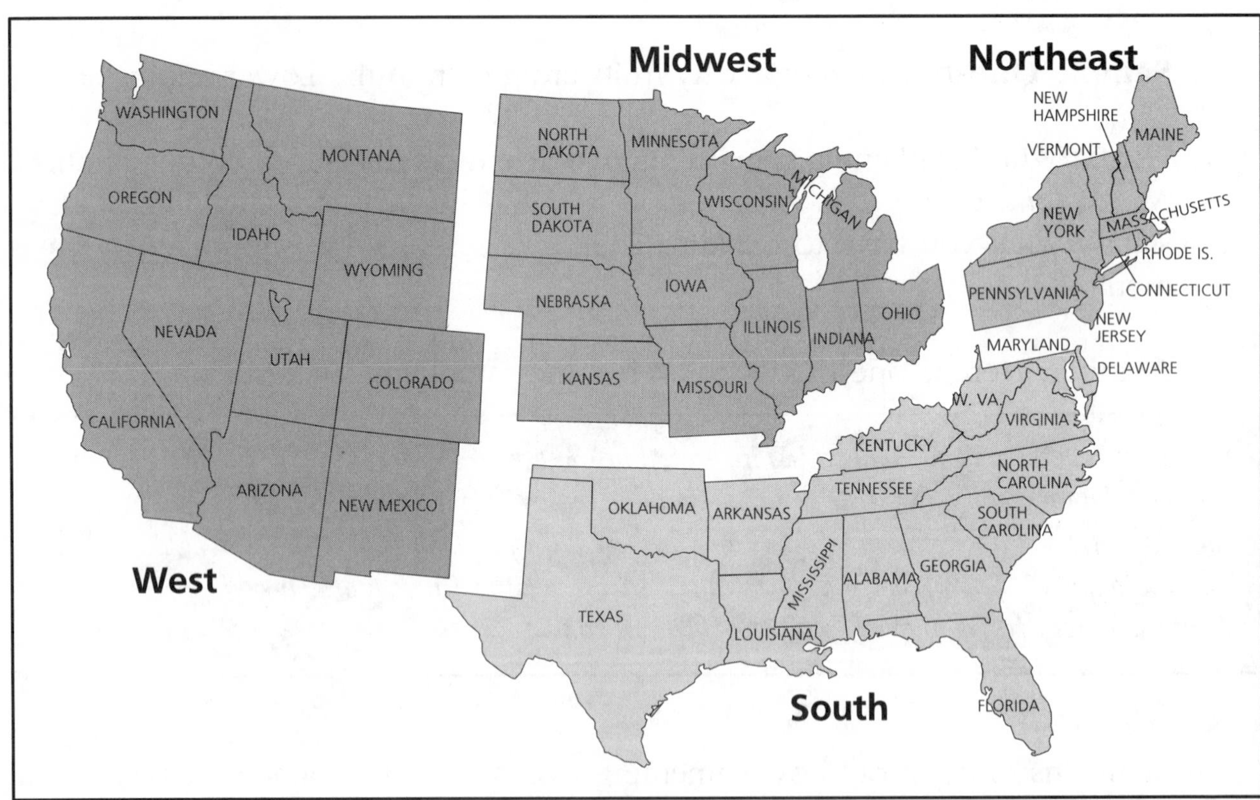

1 The states of the United States can be divided into different regions which sometimes share common characteristics.

On the lines provided, first **identify two states** from each region. Then, select one region and describe characteristics common to that region.

Identification of states in the each region:

REGIONS	NAME OF STATE	NAME OF STATE
Northeast		
Midwest		
South		
West		

Region selected: ______________________

Description of some characteristics common to that region:

____

____

____

The benchmark being tested here is to "locate and describe major places and communities of the United States." **[II.1.LE.3]**

QUESTIONS ASKING YOU TO ORGANIZE INFORMATION

Constructed-response questions may also ask you to "construct" or "make" something instead of writing a paragraph to describe, explain, or show something. For example, you might be required to fill in a table, create a graph, complete a map, or make a timeline. Each of these ways of presenting information has already been explained in Chapter 2 of this book.

Let's take a look at one sample question to give you an idea of what you might be asked to do.

A SAMPLE QUESTION

Directions: You should take about 5 minutes to read the question and study the paragraph. Use it with what you already know to complete the tasks.

Read the following paragraph:

In 1990, our national government counted the number of people living in the United States. The results of the count revealed the following information about these cities in Michigan: **Detroit's** population was 1,027,974; **Grand Rapids** was 189,126; **Warren** was 144,864; **Flint** was 140,761; **Lansing** was 127,321; **Marquette** was 21,977 and **Sault Ste. Marie** was 14,689.

Task I:
Using the information in the paragraph, fill in the second column of the table below showing the 1990 population for these seven Michigan cities.

THE POPULATION OF SEVEN MICHIGAN CITIES, 1990

City	
Detroit	
Grand Rapids	
Warren	
Flint	
Lansing	
Marquette	
Sault Ste. Marie	

Task II:
In one sentence, give a reason why Marquette and Sault Ste. Marie have smaller populations than the other cities in the table.

____

____

The benchmark being tested here asks you to "locate and describe major places, cultures, and communities of the United States." **[II.1.LE.3]**

CHAPTER 5

GEOGRAPHY

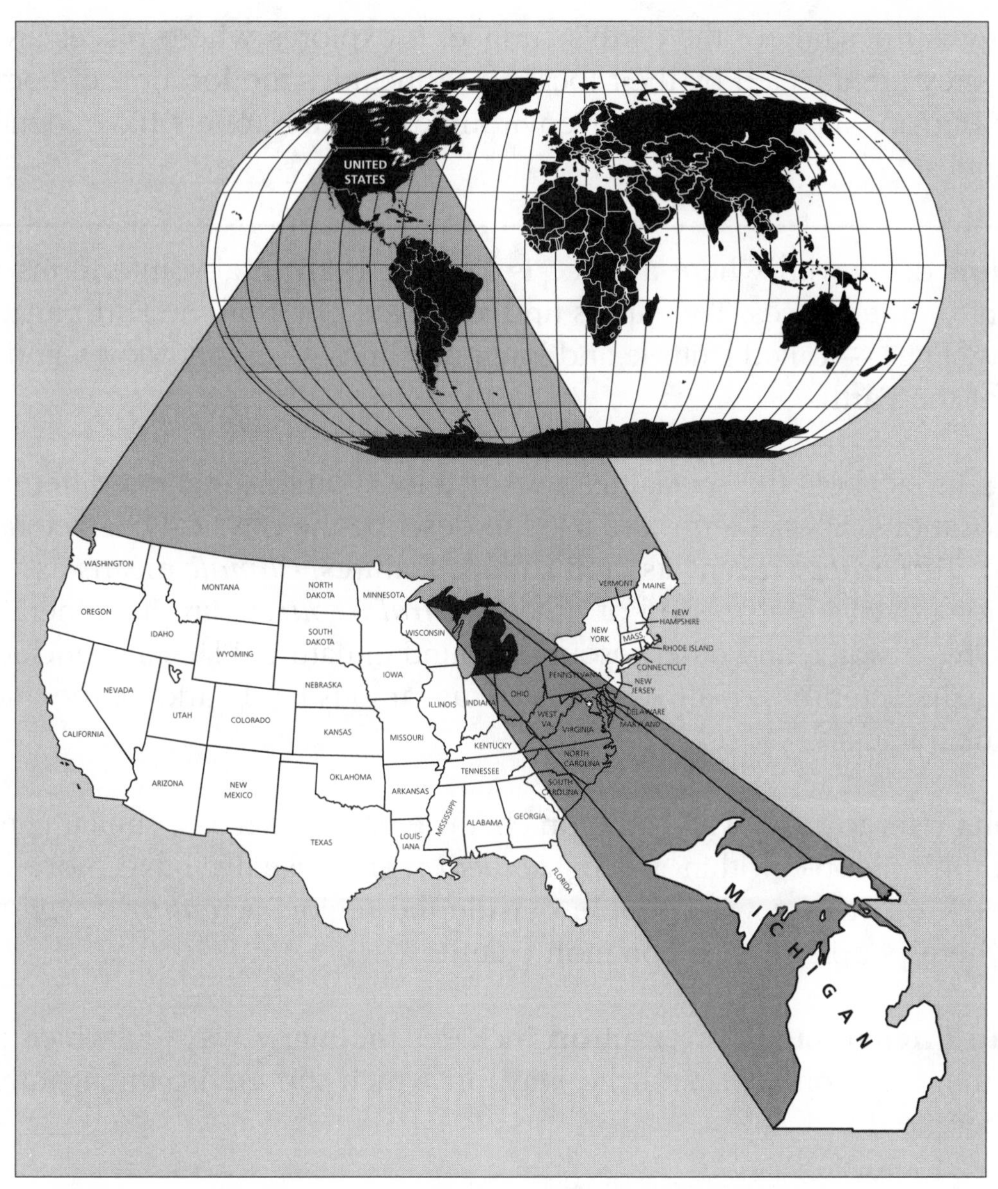

SECTION 1 A CAPSULE SUMMARY OF GEOGRAPHY

Geography is the study of the earth's surface. It explores where places are located, and how they are affected by their location. It includes the location of communities and how humans interact with their environment. Geographers have identified five major themes:

Location deals with where a place is located, both in absolute terms and in relation to other places. To help us find any fixed point on the Earth, map makers draw lines — called latitude and longitude lines — up and down and across maps of the Earth.

Place tells us about the special features of a location that make it different from other locations. Special terms are used to describe the physical characteristics of a place. *Topography* means its land surface features. *Climate* means its weather conditions over a long period of time. *Natural resources* are its minerals, soil, forests, fresh water, and other resources found in nature. Place also includes the cultural characteristics of a location, such as famous landmarks or the traditions of its inhabitants.

Regions refer to areas with common characteristics, such as a similar climate or topography. People within a *geographical region* usually have more contact with each other than with people outside the region. A *cultural region* is an area where people share a common culture.

Human-Environment Interaction includes the many ways in which people affect their environment, and the ways in which the environment influences what people do.

Movement refers to the movement of goods, services, ideas, and people from one place to another.

To do well on the Social Studies MEAP Test, you must understand:

- the physical and cultural geography of Michigan;
- the main physical and cultural regions of the United States;
- the location of the main cultures and communities of the United States; and
- the Great Lakes ecosystem.

THE PHYSICAL AND CULTURAL GEOGRAPHY OF MICHIGAN

MICHIGAN'S PHYSICAL GEOGRAPHY

Michigan consists of two separate regions: the Upper and Lower Peninsula.

- ✦ **Location.** Michigan is often called the "Great Lakes State" because it is bordered by four of the five Great Lakes and is part of the Great Lakes ecosystem. Historically, people from all over the Midwest could ship their goods to Michigan, across Lake Erie, and along the Erie Canal to New York City and the Atlantic Ocean.

- ✦ **Climate.** The state's climate is influenced by its nearness to the Great Lakes. The lakes make summers cooler and winters warmer than they otherwise would be.

- ✦ **Topography.** Michigan's land surface features were formed thousands of years ago by the action of glaciers. The highest elevation is in the western Upper Peninsula, and is called the Superior Uplands. The Lower Peninsula and eastern half of the Upper Peninsula are flat or rolling plains.

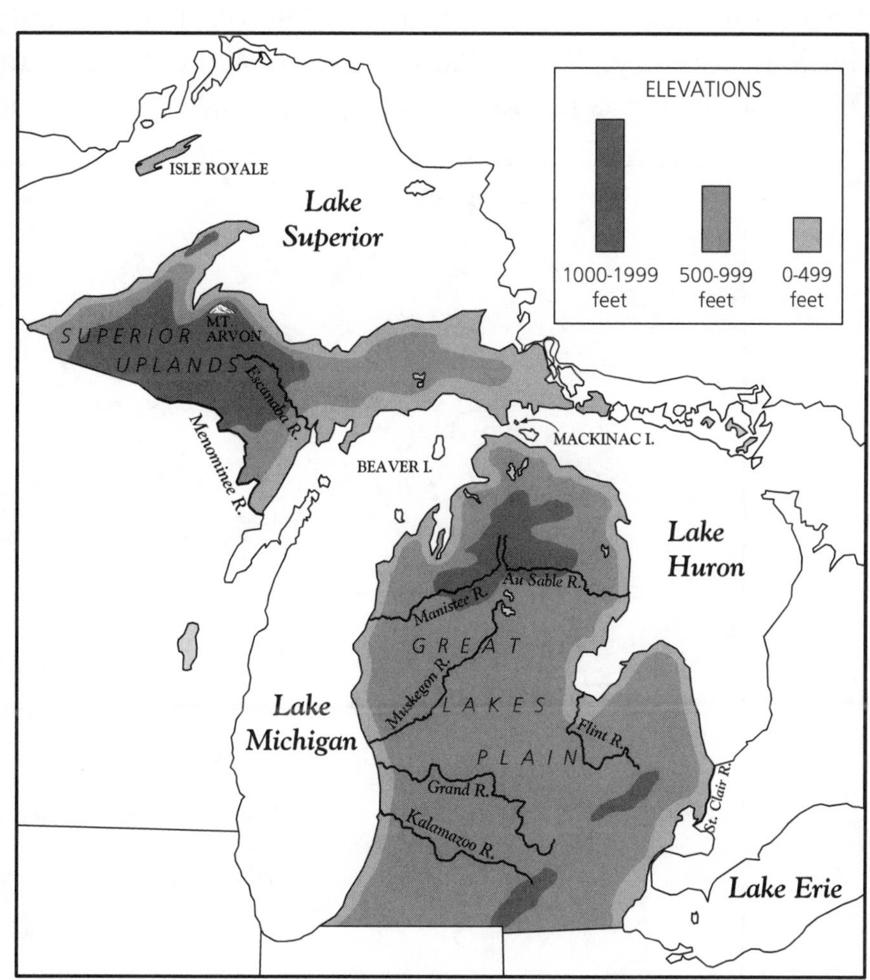

- ✦ **Bodies of Water.** Michigan has thousands of lakes, as well as hundreds of islands in the Great Lakes. It has the longest coastline of any state except Alaska.

- ✦ **Natural Resources.** Michigan's valuable natural resources include the forests of the Upper Peninsula, the fertile soil of the Lower Peninsula, and abundant fresh water in lakes, streams, and rivers. In addition, Michigan has deposits of copper and iron ore in the Upper Peninsula, oil and natural gas, salt deposits, gypsum, sand and gravel.

MICHIGAN'S CULTURAL GEOGRAPHY

The Upper Peninsula is thinly populated. Marquette and Sault St. Marie are its two largest cities. The main center of Michigan's population is the southern Lower Peninsula. Detroit, with over a million people, is the state's largest city. Other important cities in the Lower Peninsula are Grand Rapids, Ann Arbor, Jackson, Flint, Pontiac, Saginaw, Bay City, Dearborn, Holland, Battle Creek, and Muskegon. Lansing is the state capital.

People of more than 100 different racial and ethnic groups live in Michigan. There are many pockets of cultural diversity in the state. For example, many people from the Middle East live in Dearborn and Detroit. Frankenmuth is a center for people of German ancestry. Grand Rapids and Holland have many Dutch Americans. The Upper Peninsula is home to many people whose ancestors came from Scandinavia.

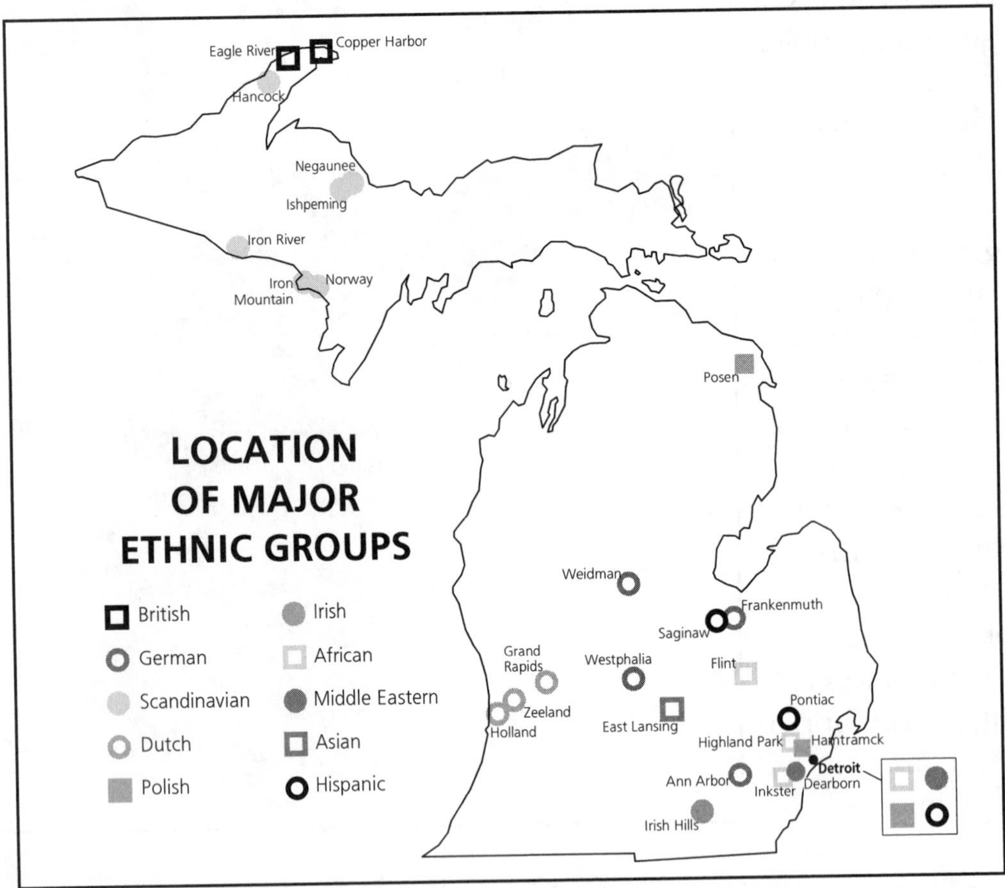

THE MAIN PHYSICAL AND CULTURAL REGIONS OF THE UNITED STATES

The world's largest land masses are called **continents**. There are seven continents — Asia, Africa, North America, South America, Europe, Australia, and Antarctica. **Regions**, on the other hand, are areas that share certain features and whose people have greater contact with places within the region than with places outside it.

PHYSICAL REGIONS OF THE UNITED STATES

A **physical region** is an area that shares similar land forms, climate, and plant and animal life. Except for the states of Alaska and Hawaii, the United States stretches from the Atlantic Ocean to the Pacific Ocean. It has five main physical regions:

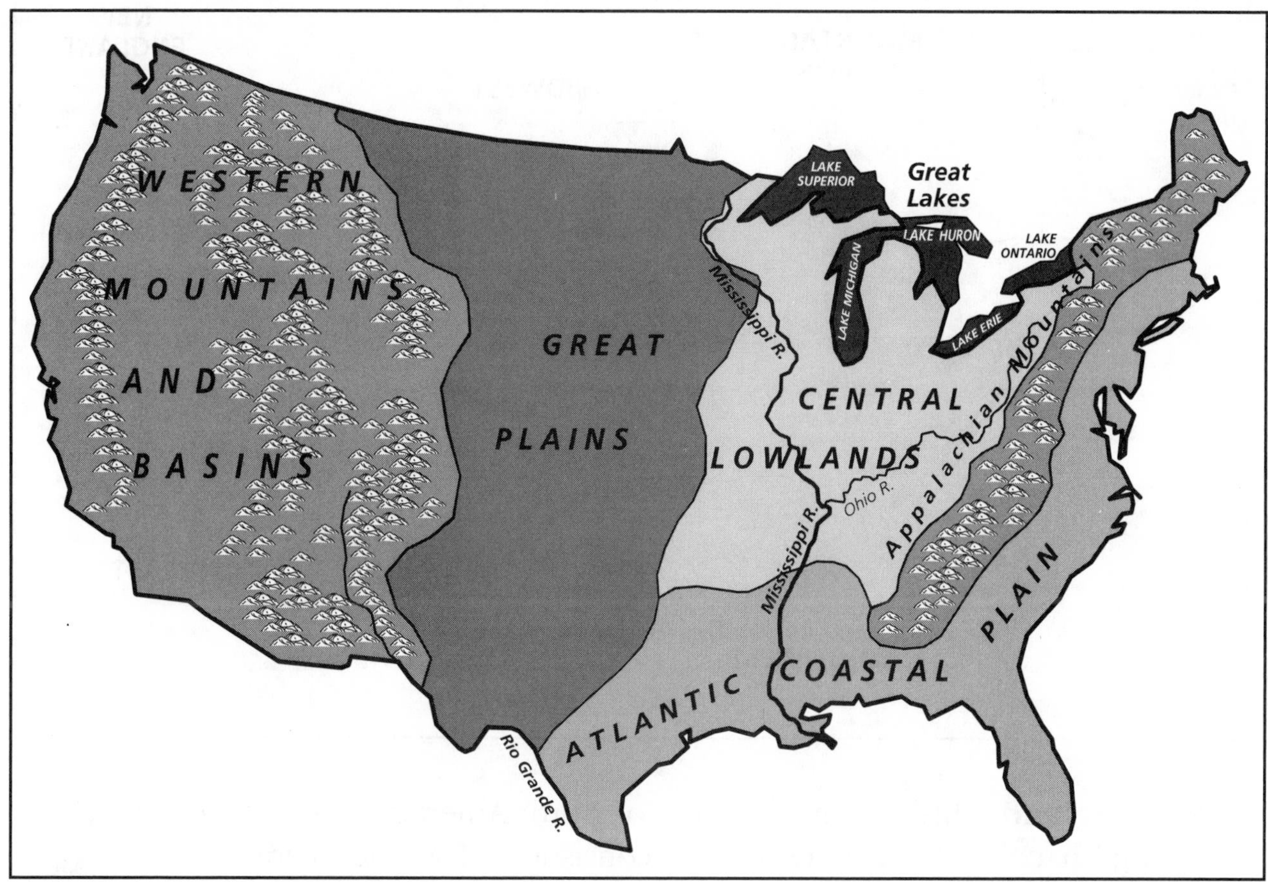

- **Atlantic Coastal Plain**. This large, fertile plain runs along the Atlantic Coast and the Gulf of Mexico. It extends west into part of Texas.

- **Appalachian Mountains**. These tree-covered mountains run several hundred miles inland — from New England in the northeast to Alabama in the south.

- **Central Lowlands**. These are flat, fertile grasslands used for farming. They produce vast amounts of food crops.

- **Great Plains**. This is an area of dry and hilly grasslands, west of the Mississippi River. The Great Plains stretch across the middle of the country and reach northward into Canada.

- **Western Mountains and Basins**. The western United States has mountainous areas such as the Rocky Mountains and the Sierra Nevada, separated by deserts, valleys and dry basins *(a basin is a low-lying area surrounded by higher lands)*.

CULTURAL REGIONS OF THE UNITED STATES

A **cultural region** is an area where people share a common **culture** — a way of life that includes language, dress, food, and customs. The United States can be divided into cultural regions in several different ways; one way is shown on the map below.

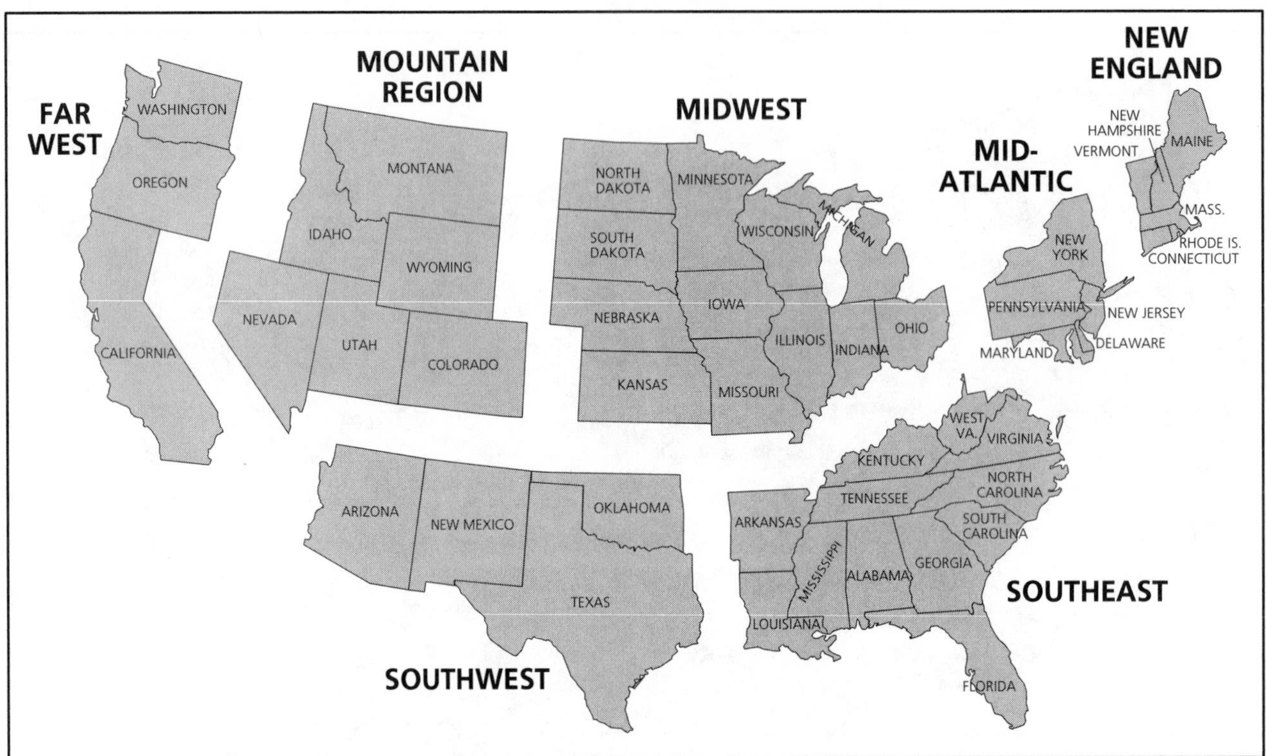

✦ **New England**. This was the first part of North America to be settled by English colonists. This region — consisting of Maine, Vermont, New Hampshire, Rhode Island, Massachusetts, and Connecticut — is now a center of education and industry. Its major cities include Boston and Providence.

✦ **Middle Atlantic States**. New York, New Jersey, Pennsylvania, Delaware and Maryland have formed an important center of commerce, industry, and culture in the United States since the mid-1800s. This region has the nation's greatest concentration of people. It includes the major cities of New York, Newark, Philadelphia and Baltimore.

✦ **Southeast**. Virginia, West Virginia, Kentucky, North and South Carolina, Tennessee, Arkansas, Kentucky, Louisiana, Mississippi, Alabama, Georgia, and Florida generally share warm and humid climates. Traditionally, people in this region grew cash crops such as rice, tobacco, and cotton. More recently, the Southeast has become a center of manufacturing for industries such as textiles. Florida is a national recreation

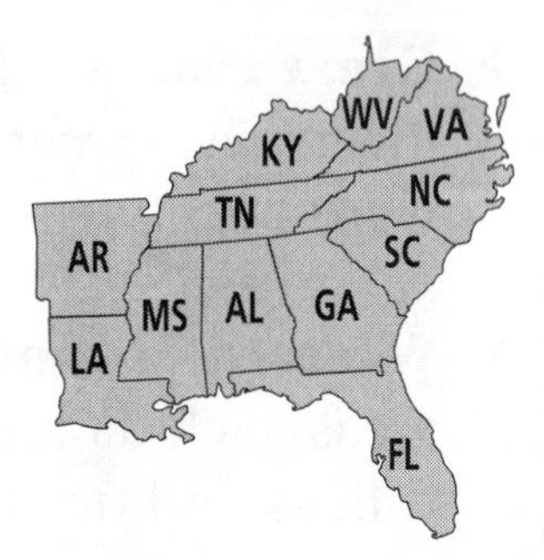

center. Major cites in the region include Charlotte, Charleston, Atlanta, Miami and New Orleans.

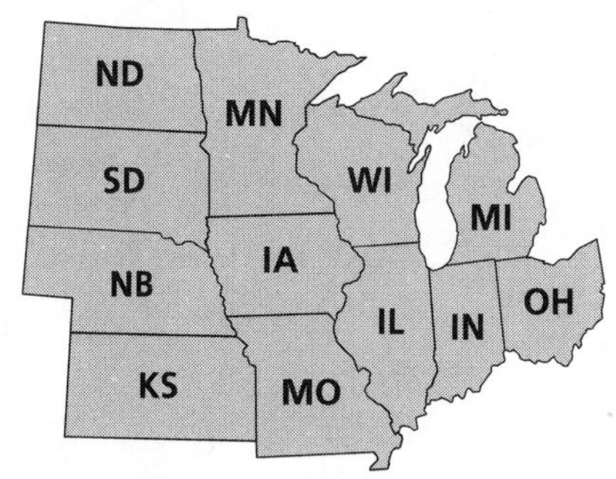

✦ **Midwest**. Ohio, Michigan, Indiana, Wisconsin, Illinois, Minnesota, Iowa, Missouri, North and South Dakota, Nebraska, and Kansas have rich farmland and heavy industries such as automobile manufacturing. The many large cities of this region include Chicago, Detroit, Green Bay, Milwaukee, Cincinnati, Columbus, Cleveland, and Gary.

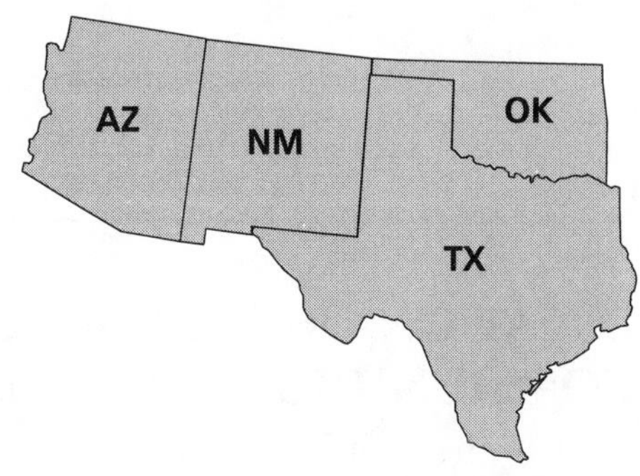

✦ **Southwest**. Oklahoma, Texas, New Mexico, and Arizona are generally dry and hot, and some areas of this region are desert. Once part of Mexico, the Southwest still shows a strong Spanish influence. With the invention of air conditioning, the population of many Southwestern cities has soared. Some major cities of the Southwest are Santa Fe, Phoenix, and El Paso. The eastern part of Texas, with the large urban areas of Houston, Dallas, and San Antonio, is sometimes considered part of the Southeast.

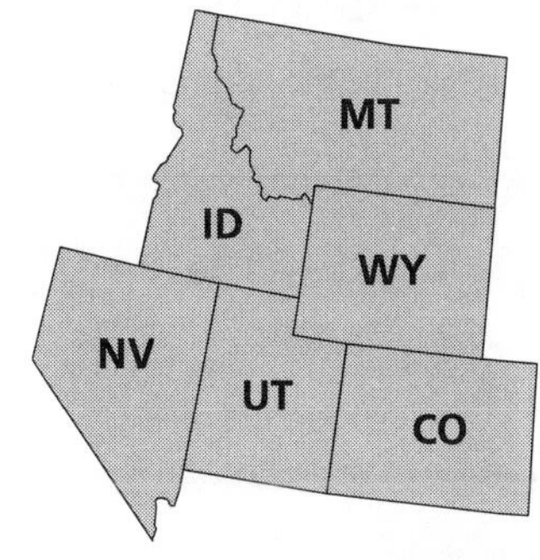

✦ **Mountain Region**. Between the Midwest and the Pacific coast states is a sparsely populated area of plains, mountains and deserts. This region consists of Montana, Wyoming, Colorado, Idaho, Utah, and Nevada. The region is famous for its natural beauty and ski resorts. Salt Lake City, Utah was settled by Mormon pioneers. Denver, Colorado first developed during the silver boom.

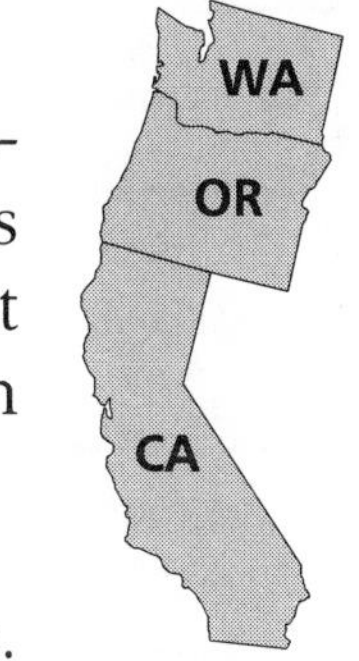

✦ **Far West**. This part of the country consists of many communities separated by large areas of open land. Along the Pacific coast are the states of Washington, Oregon, and California. California is the nation's most populated state. The region's major cities are Seattle, Portland, San Francisco, Los Angeles, and San Diego.

Alaska and Hawaii are not physically connected to the United States. Alaska is on the Pacific coast, connected to northern Canada. Hawaii is a chain of islands in the mid-Pacific. Each of these states is a cultural region of its own.

Note: *For the MEAP Test, you should be familiar with the location of the fifty states of the United States. For help with this, study the map on the next page.*

LOCATION OF THE MAIN CULTURES AND COMMUNITIES IN THE UNITED STATES

The United States is a multi-cultural society made up of people of many races, religions, and ethnic groups. Although members of nearly all cultural groups live in most parts of our nation, certain areas have particularly strong cultural influences.

Cultural Group	Where They Are Located
British (English, Welsh, Scots) and Irish	The British were the original settlers of the thirteen colonies along the Atlantic coast. From there, they moved throughout the United States. In the 1800s, Irish immigrants came to large cities like Boston and New York.
Germans	Large numbers of Germans came to the United States in the 19th century. Many of them settled in Michigan and other Midwestern states.
Spaniards and Latin Americans	Spanish colonists settled in areas that once belonged to Spain, like Florida, Texas, California, New Mexico, and Arizona. More recently, Latin Americans have migrated in large numbers to these same areas.
Southern and Eastern Europeans	Italians, Russians, Poles, Greeks, and Eastern European Jews came to New York City and other cities in the late 1800s and early 1900s. Large numbers of their descendants live today in the Northeast and Midwest.
Africans and African Americans	Africans were first forcibly brought as enslaved workers to the Southeast. In the 20th century, large numbers of African Americans migrated to cities in the Northeast and Midwest.
Asians	Chinese and Japanese immigrants came to California in the 19th century, primarily to work at building railroad lines. In more recent times, Asian immigrants have moved into cities throughout the United States.

THE GREAT LAKES ECOSYSTEM

Within a physical region, such as a rain forest, desert or prairie, there is a balanced relationship between land, water, the atmosphere, plants and animals. This balanced relationship is known as an **ecosystem** — a system in which plants, animals, and the physical environment work together as a single unit.

HOW AN ECOSYSTEM WORKS

The basis for any ecosystem is plant life. Plants trap the energy in sunlight. Plants also get nutrients from the soil, and water from rain, snow or dew. Animals then eat plants to survive. After the animals die, bacteria, worms, and insects break down the animal bodies and return their nutrients to the soil, where they are used by plants.

Energy flows from the sun to the grasses, and rain helps them grow. Rabbits feed on the grasses, and absorb their energy and nutrients. Coyotes eat some of the rabbits, and absorb their energy and nutrients. When the rabbits and coyotes die, their bodies enrich the soil for the grasses. The activities of these plants and animals can also affect land forms and climate. Grass roots prevent the soil from eroding. Grass also releases oxygen into the air for animals to breathe. Some of the carbon dioxide exhaled by animals is absorbed by the grass, and the rest traps heat in the atmosphere,

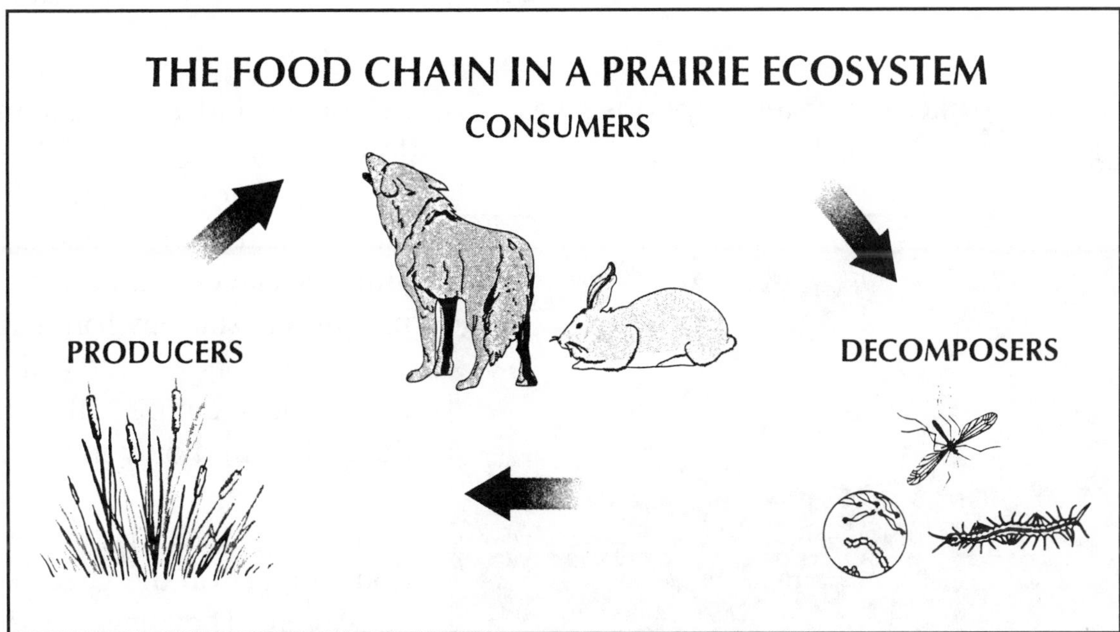

THE IMPORTANCE OF THE GREAT LAKES ECOSYSTEM

The Great Lakes ecosystem is located where the forests of the eastern United States, the pine forests of Canada and the grassy prairies of the Midwest all meet. This ecosystem includes the five Great Lakes and their surrounding areas, and extends through eight states and two Canadian provinces.

The Great Lakes dominate this ecosystem and influence its climate. The lakes were formed during an Ice Age thousands of years ago, when powerful glaciers moved across the land. The glaciers gouged out enormous holes which eventually filled with water, creating lakes. The Great Lakes hold one-fifth of all the world's fresh surface water. The region's rainfall passes into streams and rivers which drain into the lakes. Much of this water then evaporates from the lakes back into the air.

The so-called "Lake Effect" influences Michigan's temperatures. Large bodies of water like the Great Lakes take longer to heat or cool than land masses do. This makes the Great Lakes a source of heat in winter and causes them to draw in cooler air in spring and summer. In winter, cold air blowing across the lakes picks up heat and moisture, bringing increased rain or snow to a narrow belt along the eastern shoreline. In summer, the cooling effect of the lakes creates "lake breezes."

Pictured Rocks, part of the Great Lakes ecosystem

The Great Lakes ecosystem supports a vast variety of plants and animals. Many of the species (types) of fish in the lakes are unique. Along the shores of the lakes are some the world's largest freshwater sand dunes. Plants and animals have adapted to this unique coastal environment by developing new kinds of species. For example, the dune thistle is found only in this area.

Shoreline view of Lake Michigan

Humans have had a tremendous impact on the Great Lakes ecosystem. They have cut down forests for logging and cleared land to grow crops. They have fished in the lakes and rivers and built large cities and highways. Today, the Great Lakes ecosystem is a center of industry and agriculture. However, human activities, especially pollution, threaten the survival of this ecosystem.

SECTION 2 MAJOR GEOGRAPHIC TERMS AND CONCEPTS

There are many important terms and concepts associated with the study of geography. Use the following graphic organizer as a review to see if you can recall them.

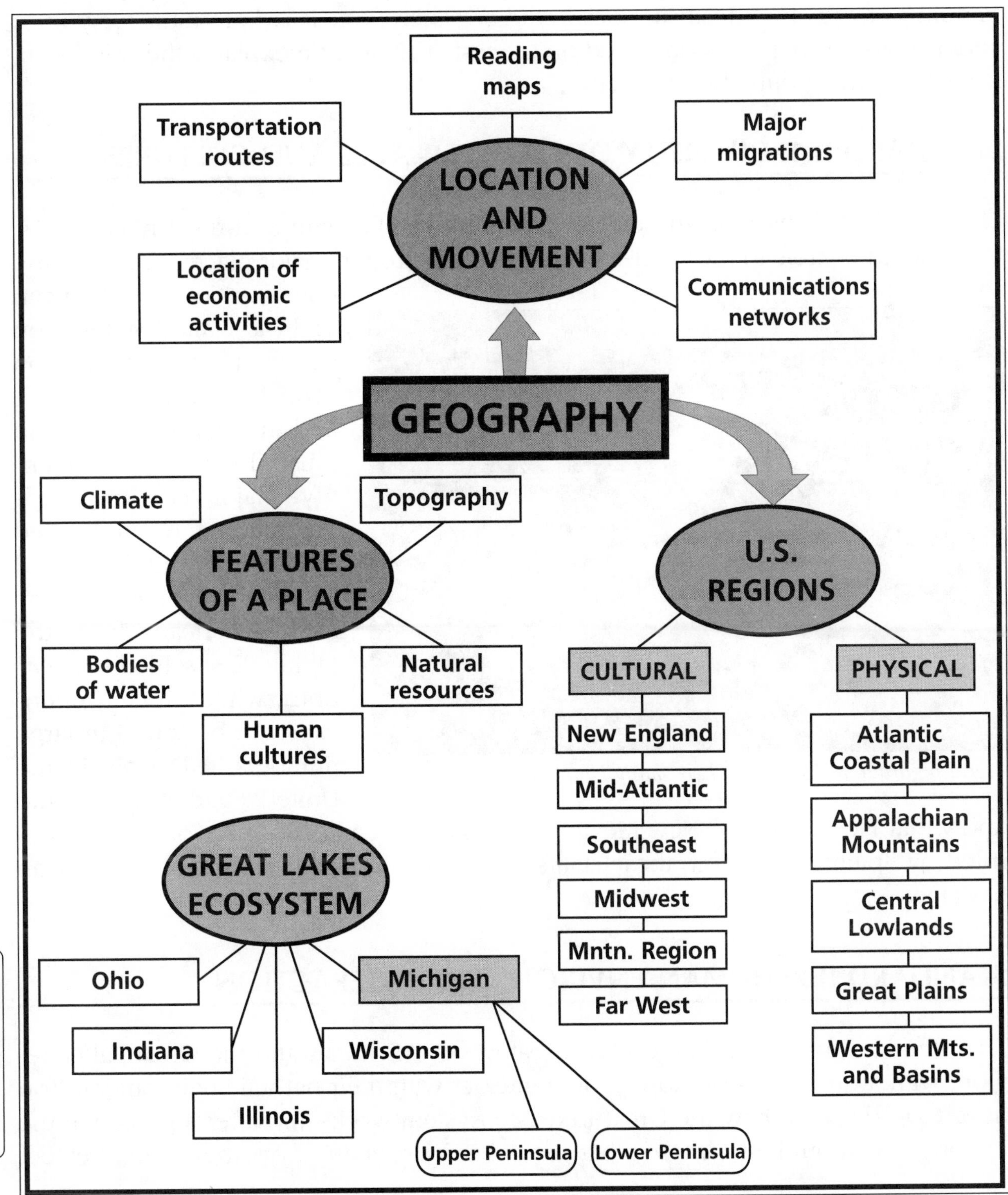

SECTION 3 THE "BIG IDEAS" IN GEOGRAPHY

In Chapter 4, you learned that it is not possible to answer MEAP Test questions correctly simply by understanding the prompt. Prompts are used to test your understanding of the "big ideas" in social studies. Therefore, it is important for you to understand the "big ideas" included on the test. This section explains the "big ideas" for geography, grouped by standard.

STANDARD II.1: DIVERSITY OF PEOPLE, PLACES AND CULTURES

This standard focuses on the cultural diversity of Michigan and the United States. You should be able to locate, describe, and compare the major places, cultures, and communities of Michigan and the United States. You should know the location of major cities in Michigan and the United States. You must also be able to identify major ethnic groups and where they are located in Michigan and the United States. For example, many Arab Americans from the Middle East settled in Dearborn, while African Americans can be found in large numbers in Detroit. In the United States, you should know that Florida, Texas, New Mexico, Arizona, and California were once territories ruled by Spain. As a result, these states have a strong Spanish and Latin American heritage.

Tulip garden in Holland, where many Dutch Americans live

STANDARD II.2: HUMAN/ENVIRONMENT INTERACTION

This standard focuses on the physical features of Michigan and the Great Lakes region, with an emphasis on how people interact with their natural environment. You need to understand how the Great Lakes ecosystem works and affects people in the region. You should also know what natural resources are, how they were created, and how they affect our activities. This standard requires you to be familiar with the major physical features of both Michigan and the United States, such as topography, ecosystems, and natural resources. You should also know how people, especially in Michigan, have adapted to their environment or modified it.

STANDARD II.3: LOCATION, MOVEMENT, AND CONNECTIONS

This standard focuses on the location of economic activities and peoples, and how these move and interact. You should know the location of major economic activities in Michigan. You should be familiar with the major migrations of people to the United States from other parts of the world. You should also know how different communities are connected through communications and transportation, and how goods, people and ideas now move through Michigan and the rest of the nation.

Ore barge moving through the Soo Locks

STANDARD II.4: REGIONS, PATTERNS, AND PROCESSES

This standard focuses on the concept of region and patterns of change. You should know the major regions of Michigan and the United States, including their location and features. You should also be able to describe how both the physical and cultural geography of Michigan have changed over time. For example, you should know how Michigan was created and affected by the movement of glaciers. You should also know how to read a map, and be able to draw maps of your community, the Great Lakes region, and the United States.

STANDARD II.5: GLOBAL ISSUES AND EVENTS

This standard requires you to know about current events and how they affect people and the environment. For example, Brazil — a country in South America — is home to the world's largest rain forest. Brazilians have been cutting down large numbers of trees in the Amazon rain forest to make new farms. The destruction of this rain forest affects people throughout the world. The Amazon rain forest produces a large amount of the world's oxygen. It also contains many unique plants and animals. Destruction of the rain forest reduces the world's oxygen supply. Such destruction often threatens many plants and animals with extinction.

PRACTICE QUESTIONS

This section contains practice selected-response and constructed-response questions about geography.

There are two clusters of selected-response questions. Each has a prompt and five questions. Examine each prompt carefully and then answer the five questions that follow it. Each question has a benchmark number to indicate what "big idea" is being tested. A detailed list of the geography benchmarks is at the end of this chapter.

There are also two constructed-response questions. Each one has a prompt and a writing task related to it. Examine each prompt carefully and then write your answers as directed.

— SELECTED-RESPONSE QUESTIONS —

Directions: Study the following map and use it with what you already know to answer the questions that follow.

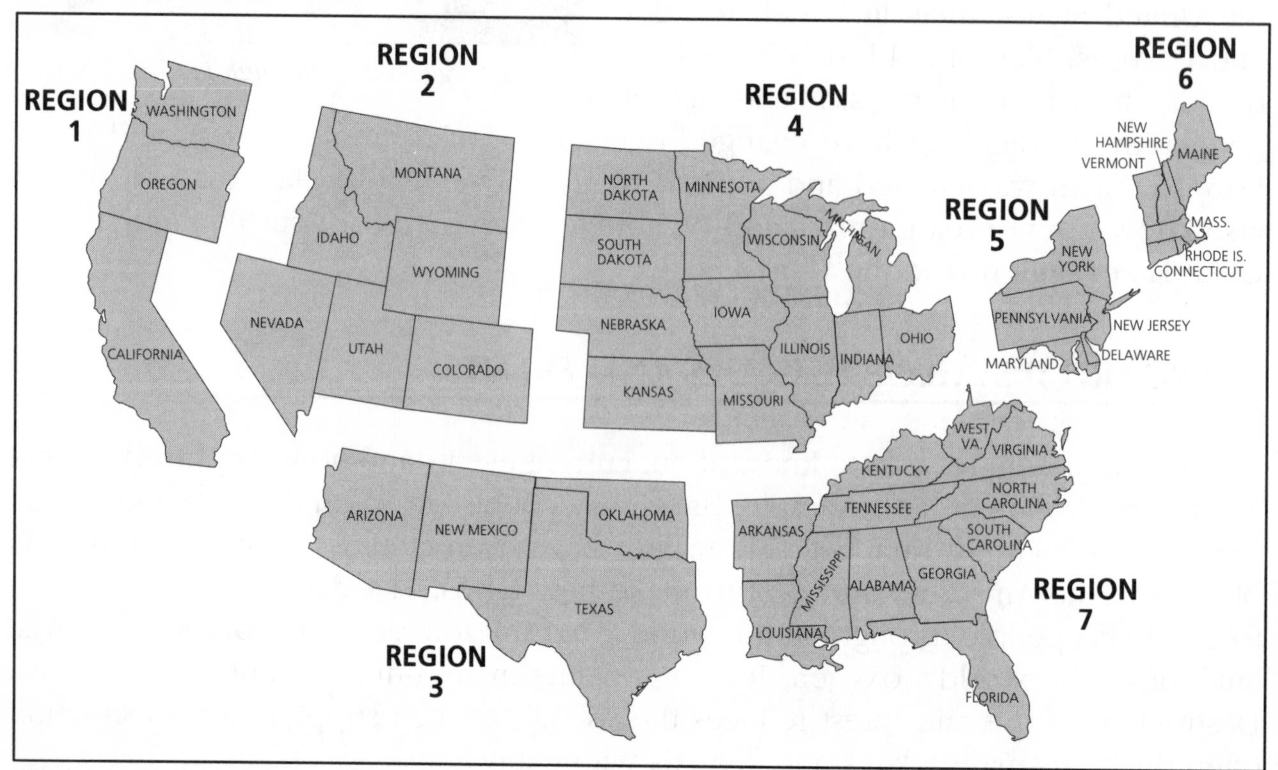

1 Which of the following regions was MOST influenced by Spanish culture?

A Region 2
B Region 3
C Region 4
D Region 6

II.4.LE.6

2 Which two regions are BEST located to trade with European countries?

A Region 5 and Region 7
B Region 4 and Region 3
C Region 1 and Region 2
D Region 3 and Region 2

II.4.LE.6

3 On which region of the United States does the Great Lakes ecosystem have the MOST impact?

A Region 4
B Region 3
C Region 2
D Region 1

II.4.LE.5

4 Immigrants coming to the United States from an Asian country to live near relatives would be MOST likely to settle in which region?

A Region 3
B Region 5
C Region 7
D Region 1

II.3.LE.2

5 In which region of the United States would rice, tobacco, and cotton be grown?

A Region 6
B Region 7
C Region 5
D Region 4

II.3.LE.1

Name ______________________ Teacher ______________________

Directions: Study the map below and use it with what you already know to answer the questions that follow.

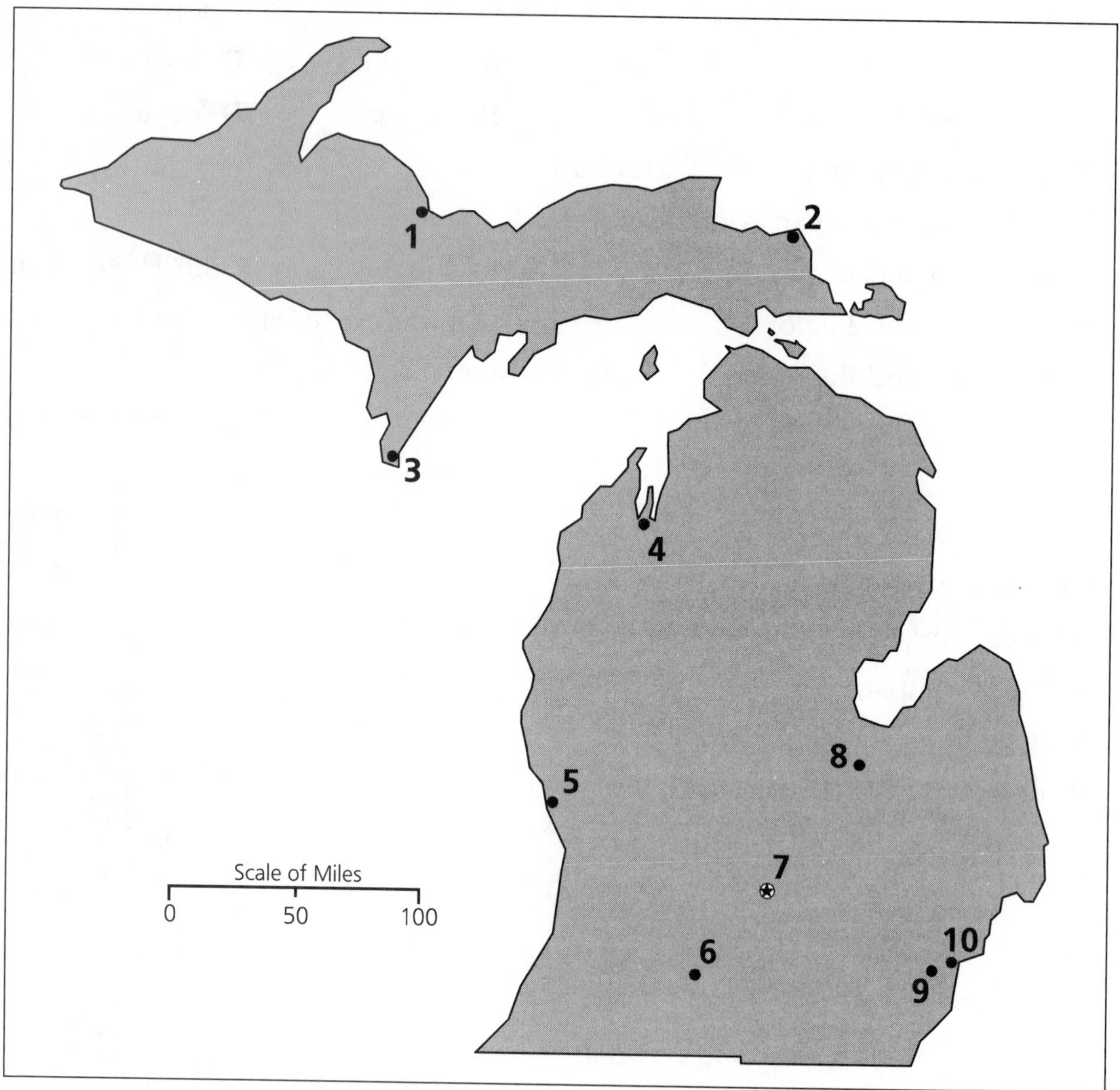

6 In which numbered Michigan city have many immigrants from the Middle East settled?

A City 1 **C** City 5

B City 3 **D** City 9

II.3.LE.2

7 If you and your family wanted to take a winter skiing vacation, which numbered city in Michigan would you be MOST likely to visit?

A City 1 **C** City 6

B City 5 **D** City 7

II.4.LE.4

8 In which numbered city did the music and automobile industries play an important role in economic development?

A City 1 **C** City 7

B City 3 **D** City 10

II.2.LE.2

9 If you wanted to establish a ferry service to Wisconsin on Lake Michigan, you would MOST likely locate your business in

A City 1 **C** City 5

B City 2 **D** City 8

II.2.LE.2

10 Which statement about the cities of Michigan is accurate?

A City 4 is the capital of Michigan.

B City 2 and City 4 are located on Lake Erie.

C City 10 has the largest population.

D City 1 and City 2 are located on Lake Michigan.

II.1.LE.2

Name ____________________ Teacher ____________________

— CONSTRUCTED-RESPONSE QUESTIONS —

Following are two constructed-response questions. Read the directions and examine each question carefully before answering. Each question has a benchmark number to show you which "big idea"" is being tested.

Directions: You should take about 5 minutes to read the following letter and use it with what you already know to complete this task.

11 You have a pen pal in China. She has written you the following letter.

Dear friend from Michigan,

Hello. How are you? I have some exciting news about coming to visit you this summer. My parents and I are planning a vacation trip to America! We have read so many things about your country. We are really interested in learning about the regions of the United States. Do you have any suggestions on what we should go see?

Your friend from China,
Ann Yen

On the line provided, identify a region in the United States. Then, complete the letter below to your pen pal. In your letter, be sure to explain some of the interesting physical and cultural features of the region you have chosen.

Identification of a region in the United States: ____________________

II.2.LE.3

Dear Ann,

I am so happy you and your family will be visiting us this summer. There are many different regions in a country as large as ours. One region that you might be interested in is

____

____

____

____

II.2.LE.1

Name ______________________ Teacher ______________________

Directions: You should take about 5 minutes to study the map and use it with what you already know to complete this task.

12 Geographic features often affect a city's development and its major economic activities. Select ONE city from either the Upper or Lower Peninsula.

On the lines provided, identify the city you selected. Then show how that city's location and natural resources played a part in its development and its major economic activities.

II.2.LE.2

City chosen: ______________________

Explanation of how that city's location and natural resources played a part in its development and its major economic activities:

Location: ____

____

Natural resources: ____

____

____

II.2.LE.2
II.4.LE.3

Name ______________________ Teacher ______________________

BENCHMARKS OF THE GEOGRAPHY STRAND

Standard II.1: People, Places and Cultures

II.1.LE.1 Locate and describe cultures and compare the similarities and differences among the roles of women, men, and families.

II.1.LE.2 Locate and describe diverse kinds of communities and explain the reasons for their characteristics and locations.

II.1.LE.3 Locate and describe the major places, cultures, and communities of the nation, and compare their characteristics.

Standard II.2: Human/Environment Interaction

II.2.LE.1 Explain basic ecosystem concepts and processes.

II.2.LE.2 Describe the location, use and importance of different kinds of resources and explain how they are created, and the consequences of their use.

II.2.LE.3 Describe the major physical patterns, ecosystems, resources and land uses of the state, region, and the country, and explain the processes that created them.

II.2.LE.4 Explain how various people and cultures have adopted to and modified the environment.

Standard II.3: Location, Movement, and Connections

II.3.LE.1 Describe major kinds of economic activity and explain the factors influencing their location.

II.3.LE.2 Describe the causes, consequences, routes, and movements of major migrations to the United States.

II.3.LE.3 Explain how transportation and communication link people and communities.

II.3.LE.4 Describe some of the major movements of goods, people, jobs, and information within Michigan and the United States and explain the reasons for the movements.

Standard II.4: Regions, Patterns, and Processes

II.4.LE.1 Draw sketch maps of the community, region, and the nation.

II.4.LE.2 Describe places, cultures, and communities in the U.S. and compare them with those in other regions and countries.

II.4.LE.3 Describe the geography of Michigan at major times in its history and explain the reasons for its change.

II.4.LE.4 Describe the physical, economic, and cultural geography of contemporary Michigan and its causes, advantages, and disadvantages.

II.4.LE.5 Describe the Great Lakes ecosystem, and explain physical and human processes that act upon them.

II.4.LE.6 Describe the geography of major U.S. regions, compare the regions, and explain the processes that created them.

Standard II.5: Global Issues and Events

II.5.LE.1 Locate major world events and explain how they impact people and the environment.

CHAPTER 6

HISTORY

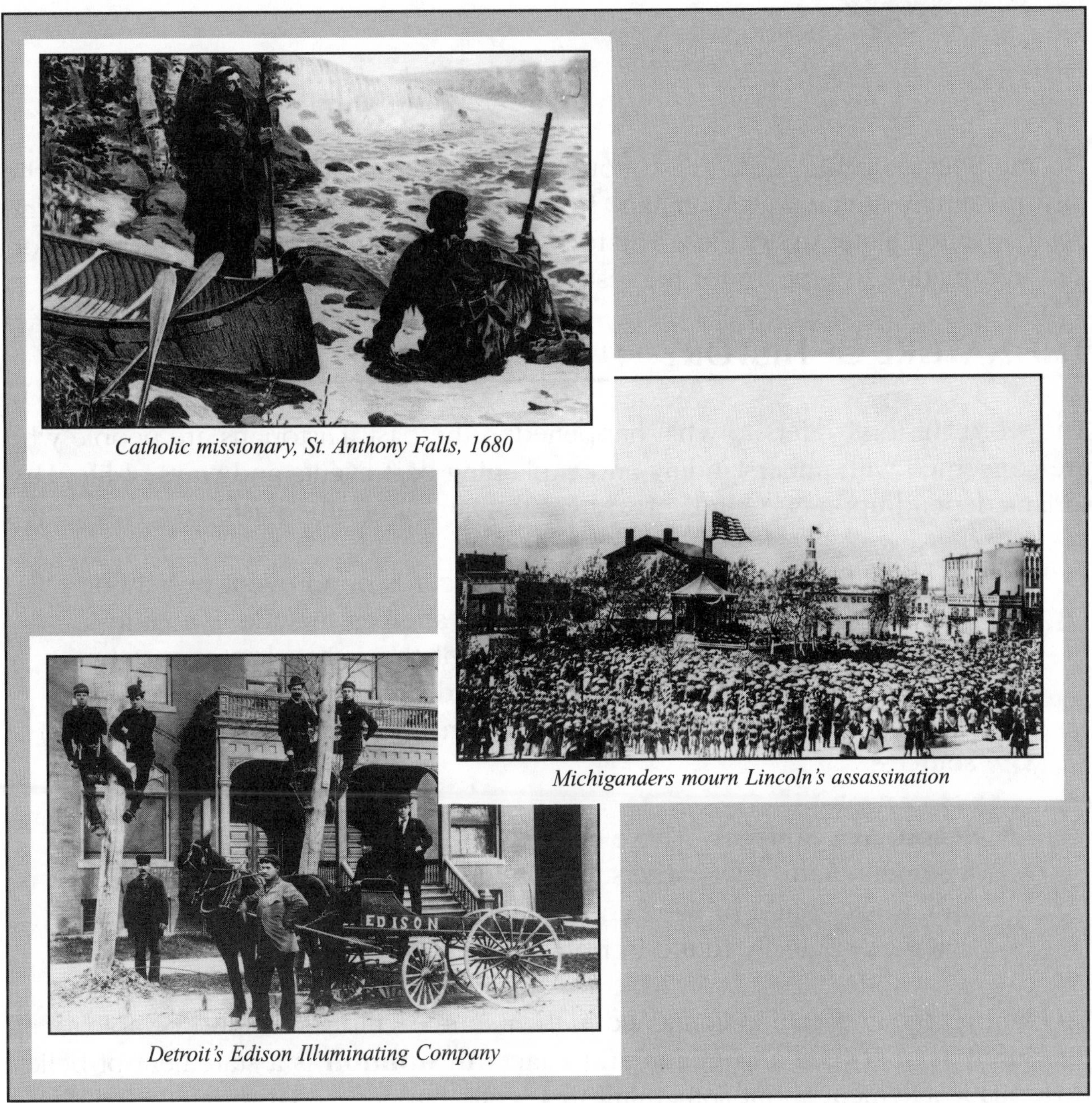

Catholic missionary, St. Anthony Falls, 1680

Michiganders mourn Lincoln's assassination

Detroit's Edison Illuminating Company

SECTION 1: A Capsule Summary of History

SECTION 2: Major Historical Terms and Concepts

SECTION 3: The "Big Ideas" in History

SECTION 4: Practice Questions

A CAPSULE SUMMARY OF HISTORY

On the Social Studies MEAP Test, you will be responsible for knowing about the history of two areas: (1) Michigan, from its beginnings up to the present, and (2) the United States up to 1763. The following summary will help you recall important information to prepare for the test.

THE NATURE OF HISTORY

The word "history" refers to what happened in the past. Historians are people who are concerned with understanding and explaining past events and ways of life. Historians depend upon two kinds of sources to learn about the past:

- ✦ **Primary Sources**. These are original records of an event or way of life that is under investigation. Primary sources include eyewitness reports, official records from the time of the event, letters sent by people involved in the event, diaries, and photographs. All historical facts used to reconstruct past events can be traced back to primary sources.

- ✦ **Secondary Sources**. These are the writings and interpretations of historians and other writers. Secondary sources such as textbooks and articles often provide convenient summaries of the information that was originally found in primary sources.

To interpret the information contained in their sources, historians must be able to tell the difference between an opinion and a fact. An **opinion** is a statement of belief. A **fact** is a statement about something that really happened. Historians often check several sources to verify *(make sure)* that a statement of fact is correct.

THE HISTORY OF MICHIGAN

The First Michiganders

Thousands of years ago, Native Americans lived in the area now known as Michigan. The first Native Americans in this area are known as "mound-builders." Later, three Native American tribes occupied the area: the Ojibwa, Ottawa, and Potawatomi. Other nearby tribes included the Huron. The tribes around the Great Lakes had similar lifestyles.

Native American setting a mink trap

Michigan Under French Rule

In 1492, **Christopher Columbus** sailed to the Americas while in search of a new trading route from Europe to Asia. Later, French explorers searched for a Northwest Passage through North America to Asia. In 1618, **Étienne Brûlé** became the first European to visit the area now known as Michigan. Later, other French explorers, missionaries, and traders arrived. For example, **Antoine de la Mothe Cadillac** started a fort at present-day Detroit in 1701. Most French settlers in Michigan were trappers and traders who obtained valuable furs from the Native Americans to ship to Europe.

The British Gain Control of Michigan

In 1754, the **French and Indian War** broke out between Great Britain and France. Many Native Americans, like Chief **Pontiac**, sided with the French, believing that British settlers would take away their land. However, the British won the war in 1763, and Michigan came under British control.

Michigan Becomes Part of the Northwest Territory

Disagreements between American colonists and the British government led to the American Revolution in 1775. The thirteen British colonies declared their independence in 1776. When the war ended in 1783, the territory of Michigan and the rest of the Great Lakes region — referred to as the **Northwest Territory** — became part of the new United States. The **Northwest Ordinance**, passed in 1787, divided the Northwest Territory into several smaller areas. It also set up a way for these areas to be admitted into the United States as equal states once they became more populated.

Michigan's Road to Statehood

Michiganders helped defend their territory during the **War of 1812**. The completion of the Erie Canal in 1825 increased the flow of settlers into Michigan. By 1835, Michigan had enough settlers to become a state. But statehood was delayed for two years when both Michigan and Ohio claimed an area south of Lake Erie known as the **Toledo Strip**. The U.S. Congress eventually awarded the Toledo Strip to Ohio, but gave Michigan the Upper Peninsula. Michigan became a state in 1837.

The first State Capitol under construction

Michigan and the Civil War

Michiganders played an important role in opposing slavery before the Civil War. **Sojourner Truth**, a famous African-American **abolitionist** *(person who fought to end slavery)*, settled in Battle Creek. Other Michiganders were active in the **Underground Railroad**, a network of "safe houses" and escape routes that helped slaves who were fleeing from the South. Michigan's proximity to Canada made it an important stop along the escape route. Later, Michiganders fought on the side of the North during the Civil War.

Sixth Michigan Cavalry charging a Confederate position, July 1863

Economic Changes Come to Michigan

The 1800s were a time of economic change for Michigan. Copper and iron deposits were discovered on the Upper Peninsula. Michigan soon led the country in copper mining. Completion of the **Soo Locks** in 1855 helped mining companies ship iron ore across the Great Lakes. Cities like Grand Rapids emerged as important furniture-making

Grand Rapids in 1900

centers. **Will Kellogg** and **Charles Post** made Battle Creek the breakfast capital of the world. Logging also became a major industry.

The Auto Industry in Michigan

Automobiles were luxury items until **Henry Ford** introduced the Model T in 1908. Ford's goal was to produce cars that most Americans could afford. He later introduced the assembly-line production of cars and doubled his workers' wages. Other major car manufacturers emerged in Michigan, such as General Motors and Chrysler. Detroit became the center of the nation's automobile industry. Their workers organized into labor unions such as the **United Auto Workers (U.A.W.).**

Ford's fifteen-millionth automobile

Michigan in Troubled Times

In 1919, the United States entered World War I in Europe. Michigan's factories began producing war goods. Many African Americans came to Michigan from the South during the **Great Migration**. In the 1920s, after the war, Michiganders enjoyed a period of good times. This was cut short when the Stock Market Crash of 1929 led to the **Great Depression**. Banks and businesses closed, and millions of Michiganders lost their jobs, savings, and homes. Just when the Great Depression seemed to be over, the United States entered World War II. From 1941 until 1945, Michiganders helped the U.S. and its allies to win the war.

Michigan in More Recent Times

The years since World War II brought many changes to Michigan. The completion of the Mackinac Bridge in 1957 connected the Upper and Lower Peninsulas. New roads and colleges were built throughout the state. Suburbs developed outside of cities. African Americans and other minority groups won greater civil rights.

Hart Plaza, Detroit — a symbol of the new Michigan

In the 1970s, Michigan's auto industry faced competition from overseas. Car sales decreased and unemployment rose. In the 1980s, Michigan's auto makers responded by making better cars, and the state's economy improved. Michigan also became a favorite recreation area. Communications and transportation advances bring new hopes for the state's future.

THE HISTORY OF THE UNITED STATES TO 1763

MAJOR NATIVE AMERICAN GROUPS

Thousands of years ago, nomadic peoples began crossing over a land bridge from Asia to North America. By the 16th century, there were 2½ million Native Americans in the area north of Mexico. They had complex cultures and different ways of life. Many different Native American tribes settled in the area that is now the United States.

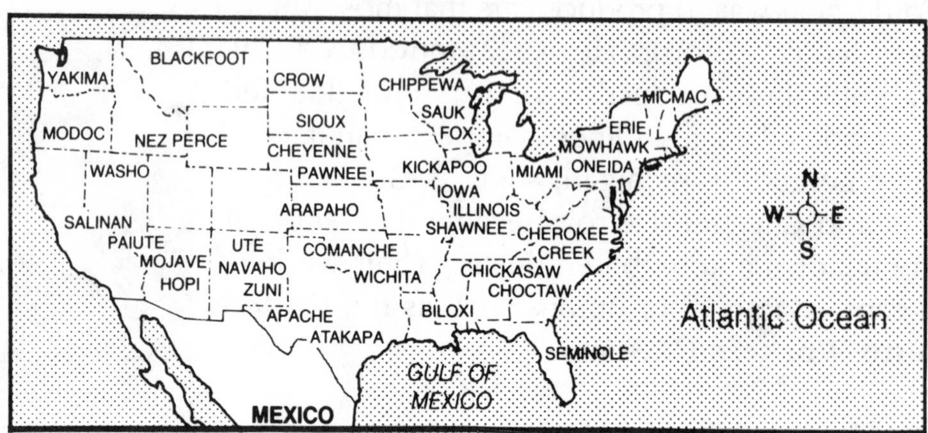

THE EUROPEANS COME TO AMERICA

About 500 years ago, new technologies in navigation, such as the compass, made it possible for Europeans to sail around the globe. The overland travels of missionaries and traders had sparked an interest in goods from East Asia. Europeans now looked for a faster way to get there — by sea.

Two European countries, Portugal and Spain, sent explorers to seek new routes to Asia. Sailing west across the Atlantic, Christopher Columbus and later explorers reached the Americas, a continent they had not known about before. They called it the "New World." Spanish and Portuguese conquerors, missionaries, and colonists followed the explorers. Many came to the Americas in search of gold and silver. Others hoped to convert the Native Americans to Christianity.

Columbus landing in the "New World"

Spain's creation of a large, powerful empire in the New World increased England and France's desire for colonies. French explorers searching for a Northwest Passage to East Asia established the colony of New France in Canada, the Great Lakes, and the Mississippi Valley. Later French settlers profited from the fur trade. English colonies were founded south of Canada, along the Atlantic coast.

COLONIAL AMERICA

The first successful English colony was started at Jamestown, Virginia, in 1607. Soon, the colony became profitable by growing tobacco for sale in England and Europe. Meanwhile, Pilgrims and Puritans established colonies in Massachusetts where they could practice their religion freely. By the mid-1730s, the thirteen English colonies had spread along the entire Atlantic coast. Soon after, different patterns of life began to develop in three separate regions:

The English land at Jamestown, Virginia,

New England. The colonies of New England — New Hampshire, Massachusetts, Connecticut and Rhode Island — had less fertile land and were colder than the other colonies. Most of the early settlers there were Puritans. New Englanders had small farms where they grew crops for their own use. Many people who lived in this area became sailors, merchants, or fishermen.

The Middle Colonies. The colonies of New York, New Jersey, Pennsylvania, Delaware and Maryland were located between New England and the Southern Colonies. Winters were not as harsh as in New England and the summers were longer. Uncleared forests and fertile soils attracted many settlers to this area. People were also attracted to these colonies by the desire for religious freedom.

The Southern Colonies. The climate of the Southern Colonies —

Virginia, North Carolina, South Carolina and Georgia — was warmer than in other parts of colonial America. The soil was well-suited to growing crops. Some Southerners developed large plantations that grew tobacco, cotton, rice and indigo (*blue dye*) for shipment to England in exchange for manufactured goods. Most of the owners of larger plantations purchased enslaved people who had been brought from Africa against their will, and used them to grow the cash crops. Slaves were not paid for their work, and were punished or killed if they tried to escape from the plantation.

Enslaved people were bought and sold as "property," often at slave auctions as depicted in this painting.

THE GROWTH OF ENGLISH TERRITORY AND POWER

New France had spread south from Canada into the Mississippi and Ohio valleys, while the English colonies were expanding westward toward New France. Eventually this led the two powerful European countries to clash with each other. France and England fought several times in the 1700s for control of the seas and overseas colonies.

The last of these struggles was known as the **French and Indian War**, which began in 1754. The Native Americans, who were caught in the middle of the conflict, generally sided with the French. The tribes feared that the British were more likely to take away their lands and destroy their way of life. An Ottawa chief named Pontiac gathered together other Native American tribes and launched a successful attack on the British at Fort Michilimackinac. They went on to capture all the forts except Fort Pontchartrain in Detroit, in what became known as "Pontiac's War."

The attack on Fort Michilimackinac

In 1759, the British General James Wolfe defeated French forces led by General Montcalm on the Plains of Abraham outside Quebec. This victory gave the British control of the St. Lawrence River. In 1763, the French surrendered Canada and the Mississippi Valley to the British in the treaty that ended the war.

SECTION 2

MAJOR HISTORICAL TERMS AND CONCEPTS

There are many important terms and concepts in history. Use this graphic organizer to review their meanings.

HISTORY

HISTORICAL INTERPRETATIONS
- Primary Sources
- Secondary Sources
- Facts
- Opinions

TIME FRAMES
- Timeline
- Chronological Order
- Decade
- Century

THE UNITED STATES BEFORE 1763
- Native Americans
- European Explorers
- New France
- 13 English Colonies
- French and Indian War

MICHIGAN

BEFORE STATEHOOD
- French Explorers
- French and Indian War
- Northwest Territory
- War of 1812
- Toledo Strip

CIVIL WAR
- Abolitionists
- Underground Railroad
- Defending the Union

INDUSTRIALIZATION
- Soo Locks
- Lumber Industry
- Mining Industry
- Auto Industry

20th CENTURY
- World War I
- Great Depression
- World War II
- Civil Rights Movement

SECTION 3

THE "BIG IDEAS" IN HISTORY

As you know, it is not possible to answer questions on the MEAP Test by simply understanding the prompts. Prompts are used to test your understanding of the "big ideas" or benchmarks. Therefore, it is important for you to understand what each standard requires for the test. The following section lists the "big ideas" for history, grouped by standard.

STANDARD I.1: TIME AND CHRONOLOGY

This standard emphasizes chronology. You should be able to measure time by 10-year periods, known as **decades**, and 100-year periods, called **centuries**. You should also be able to identify *when* major events occurred in the history of Michigan and early America (to 1763). For example, could you place these events in correct chronological order: the settling of Massachusetts by English colonists, the introduction of Ford's Model T, Michigan statehood, and completion of Detroit's Renaissance Center?

STANDARD I.2: COMPREHENDING THE PAST

This standard focuses on past events and lifestyles. For example, you may read a short passage about life among early pioneers in the Northwest Territory. Then you would be asked to put events in the passage into chronological order. Or you might have to read narratives and interpret graphs about Michigan's past. You might also be asked to compare past and present-day lifestyles in the same places in Michigan. For example, you might be shown a picture of the inside of an Ojibwa wigwam and be asked how various objects there met human needs that people still have today. This standard also requires you to be able to tell brief life stories of some past Michiganders and Americans from other parts of the United States. You should be able to identify how some of these individuals showed qualities of good character and personal virtue.

Wigwam made of birch bark

STANDARD: I.3 ANALYZING AND INTERPRETING THE PAST

This standard focuses on how to use primary sources to reconstruct past events. Primary sources are original records of events, such as letters, documents, or eyewitness descriptions. You should be able to use primary sources to piece together an account of past events or lifestyles. Often, different primary sources will give conflicting views. For example, you might be given a letter by Christopher Columbus describing his first meeting with the Native Americans in 1492, and be asked how a Native American's description of the same event might be different. Finally, questions on this standard may require you to narrate stories of key events in the history of Michigan and the early United States.

Native Americans observing a European ship

STANDARD: I.4 JUDGING DECISIONS FROM THE PAST

This standard asks you to re-evaluate decisions made in the past. You should be able to take a problem that once divided Michiganders or Americans and describe the interests and values of the people involved. For example, before the Civil War, abolitionists believed slavery was wrong and that a person could not be owned like a piece of property. Southern slave owners believed that slaves were their private property. They said abolitionists had no right to interfere in their way of life and that their slaves often received better treatment than Northern factory workers. In an actual test question, you might be given a letter by an abolitionist and be asked to explain the interests and values of the slaves, slaveowners, or abolitionists.

Slaves on a Southern plantation carrying cotton

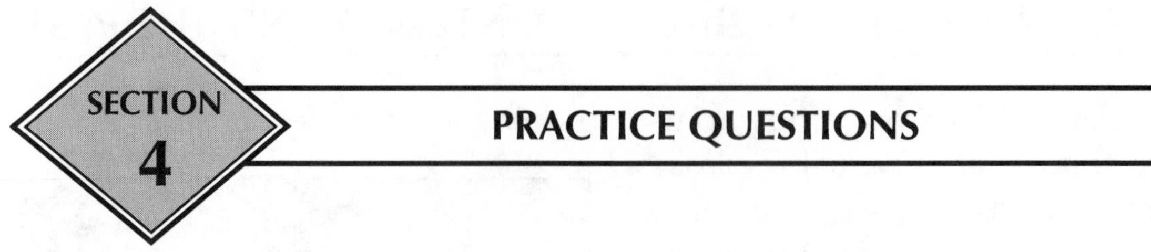

— SELECTED-RESPONSE QUESTIONS —

The following selected-response questions contain two prompts with five questions for each prompt. Examine each prompt carefully and then answer the questions that follow. Each question has a benchmark number to indicate what "big idea" is being tested. A list of the history benchmarks is at the end of this chapter.

Directions: Study the following timeline and use it with what you already know to answer the questions that follow.

1895	1902	1903	1908	1914	1925
	Cadillac Motor Company orga-nized		General Motors founded		Chrysler Motors estab-lished

1 How many decades are represented on this timeline?

A two **C** four

B three **D** five

I.1.LE.1

2 Which of the following is an historical fact?

A General Motors makes the best automobiles.

B Chrysler Motors was established 17 years after General Motors.

C Cadillac was organized 12 years before General Motors.

D Cadillac Motor Company is better than General Motors or Chrysler Motors because it came first.

I.1.LE.2

3 Which person's achievements would MOST likely be placed on the timeline?

A Charles W. Post

B Henry Ford

C Lewis Cass

D Joe Louis

I.1.LE.3

4 Which event came AFTER the time period covered in the timeline?

A Gerald Ford became President of the United States.

B Michigan was admitted as a state in the United States.

C Sojourner Truth spoke out against slavery.

D The Civil War started.

I.1.LE.2

5 What would be the BEST title for the events on this timeline?

A The History of the Automobile

B Key Events in Michigan's Automobile Industry

C Michigan in the 18th and 19th Centuries

D The United States at the Turn of the 20th Century

I.2.LE.1

Name ______________________ Teacher ______________________

Directions: Study the following illustration and use it with what you already know to answer the questions that follow.

Historians often need to "see" places from the past. Sometimes a model helps us to imagine how a place really looked. The illustration below shows Fort Michilimackinac when it was under British control.

FORT MICHILIMACKINAC*

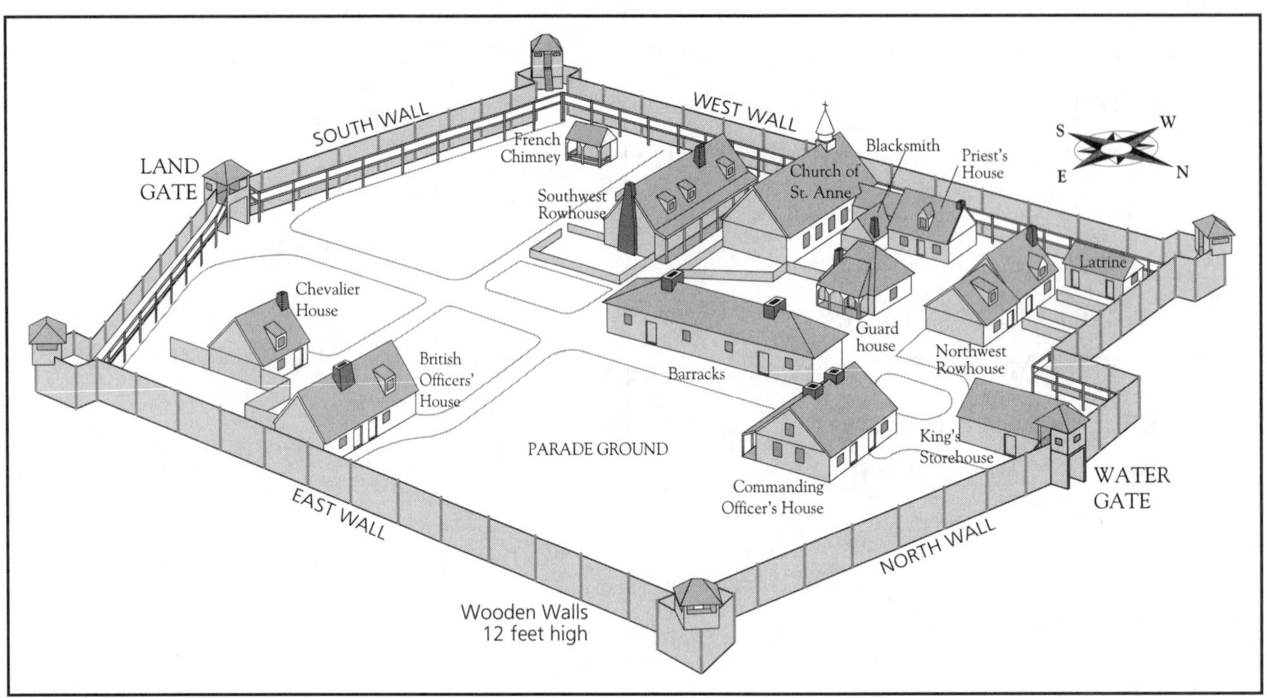

*The fort was originally built by the French in 1715.

6 In the year 2015, how old will the fort depicted by the model be?

A one century **C** fifteen decades

B six decades **D** three centuries

I.1.LE.1

7 What advantage did the fort's high walls have for the British?

A protection from attack by Native Americans

B shelter from frequent storms in the area

C protection from raids by the Russians

D safety for storing gold and other precious metals

I.2.LE.1

8 Which of the following would be a primary source that helped in the construction of the model depicted?

A a recent photograph of Fort Michilimackinac

B a book about forts built in Michigan

C a magazine article written by a leading Michigan architect

D blueprints of the original fort

I.3.LE.1

9 Which of the following is a FACT that can be determined from a careful examination of the illustration?

A Chevalier House was where the commander of the fort lived.

B Corn was grown inside the fort to help feed the soldiers.

C The walls of Fort Michilimackinac were over 10 feet high.

D Over 2,000 people lived in Fort Michilimackinac.

I.3.LE.2

10 Which of the following would MOST likely have lived in the fort when it was under French control?

A a logger

B a miner

C a fur trader

D a farmer and his family

I.2.LE.3

Name ______________________ Teacher ______________________

— CONSTRUCTED-RESPONSE QUESTIONS —

The following section has two constructed-response questions. Read the directions and examine each question carefully before answering. Each question has a corresponding benchmark number to show you what "big idea" is being tested.

Directions: You should take about 5 minutes to read the following material and use it with what you already know to complete this task.

11 Since the mid-1800s, Michigan has been one of the most productive states in the United States. Some of the major industries to develop in Michigan in the last 150 years are illustrated below.

On the lines provided, choose **one** of these industries. For the industry selected, identify the area in the state where it originally developed. Then describe the industry and explain how its economic activities affected the people of Michigan.

Name ______________________________ Teacher ______________________________

Identification of an industry and where it developed:

Industry: ______________________________

Location in the state: ____

I.1.LE.2

Description of the industry and how its economic activities affected the people of Michigan:

____

____

____

____

____

____

____

____

____

____

____

I.2.LE.2\
I.2.LE.3

Name ______________________________ Teacher ______________________________

Directions: You should take about 5 minutes to read the following material and use it with what you already know to complete this task.

12 The editors of a history magazine asked a group of historians to consider the following: Name one scene or incident in American history you would like to have witnessed, and explain why. One historian answered as follows:

> "I would like to have been on the Plains of Abraham on the morning of September 13, 1759, when General Wolfe's British army met and defeated Montcalm's French forces. Rarely has a single battle proved so decisive to history. This victory of the British over the French had a great impact on the future of North America. It was significant because ..."
>
> *Franklin B. Wickwire*

How would Mr. Wickwire have been likely to finish his answer? On the lines provided, identify the war in which the battle was fought and describe what the war was about. Then explain why the battle of September 13, 1759 was so important.

Identification of the war and description of what it was about:

____

____

____

Explanation of why the battle was so important:

____

____

____

____

____

I.3.LE.3

Name ______________________ Teacher ______________________

BENCHMARKS OF THE HISTORY STRAND

Standard I.1: Time and Chronology

I.1.LE.1 Measure chronological time by decades and centuries.

I.1.LE.2 Place major events in the development of their local community and the state of Michigan in chronological order.

I.1.LE.3 Place major events in the early history of the United States in chronological order.

Standard I.2: Comprehending The Past

I.2.LE.1 Summarize the sequence of key events in stories describing life from the past in their local community, the state of Michigan, and other parts of the United States.

I.2.LE.2 Use narratives and graphic data to compare the past of their local community, the state of Michigan, and other parts of the United States with present-day life in those places.

I.2.LE.3 Recount the lives and characters of a variety of individuals from the past representing their local communities, the state of Michigan and other parts of the United States.

I.2.LE.4 Identify and explain how individuals in history demonstrated good character and personal virtue.

Standard: I.3 Analyzing and Interpreting the Past

I.3.LE.1 Use primary sources to reconstruct past events in their local community.

I.3.LE.2 Interpret conflicting accounts in both Michigan and United States history and analyze the viewpoints of the authors.

I.3.LE.3 Compose simple narratives of events from the history of the state of Michigan and of the United States.

Standard: I.4 Judging Decisions from the Past

I.4.LE.1 Identify problems from the past that divided their local community, the state of Michigan, and the United States and analyze the interests and values of those involved.

I.4.LE.2 Select decisions made to solve problems and evaluate those decisions in terms of ethical considerations, the interests of those affected by the decisions and the short and long term consequences of those decisions.

CHAPTER 7

ECONOMICS

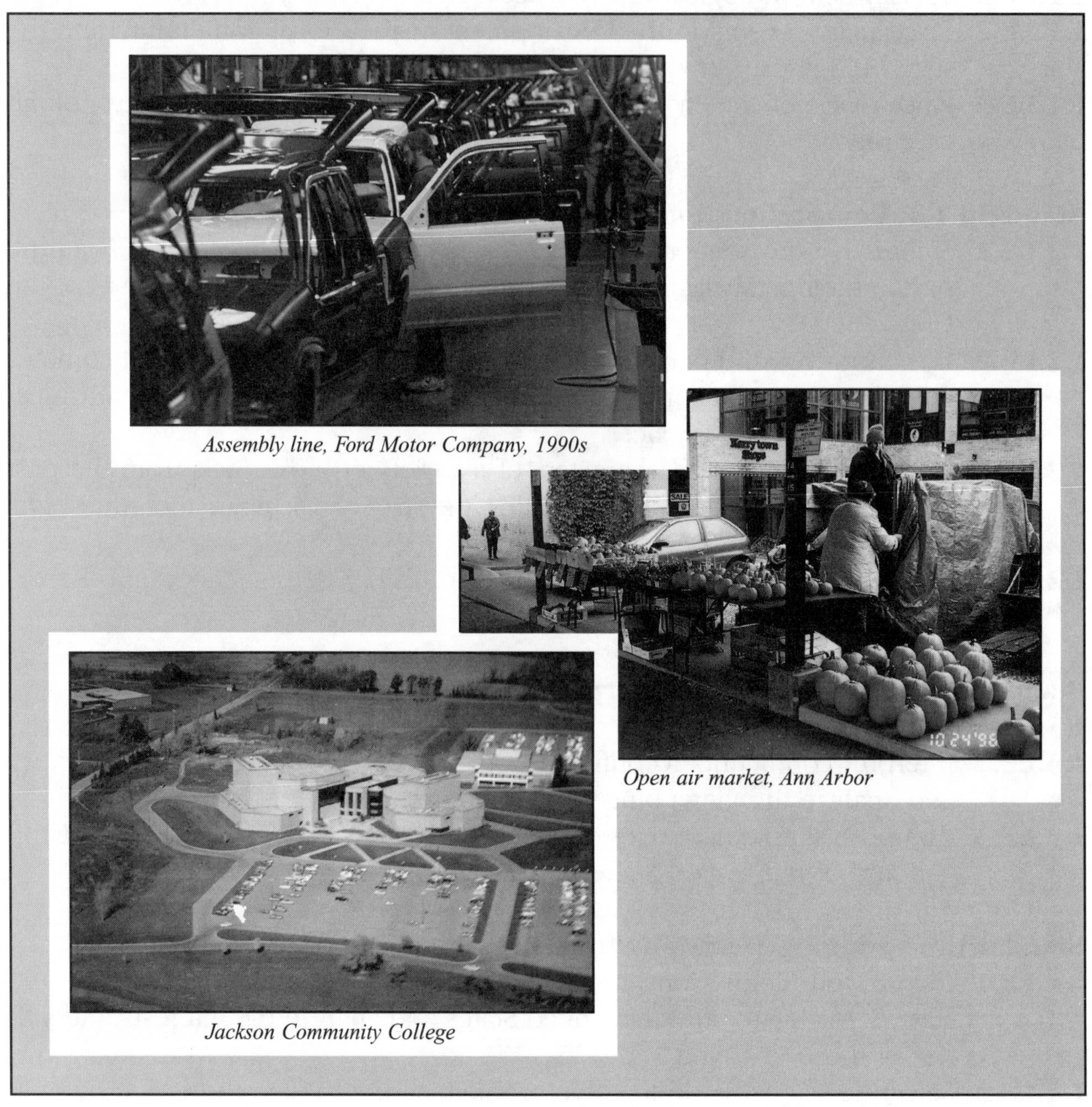

Assembly line, Ford Motor Company, 1990s

Open air market, Ann Arbor

Jackson Community College

Section 1: A Capsule Summary of Economics

Section 2: Major Economics Terms and Concepts

Section 3: The "Big Ideas" in Economics

Section 4: Practice Questions

A CAPSULE SUMMARY OF ECONOMICS

The Social Studies MEAP Test in will examine your knowledge of general economic concepts. To prepare for the test, review the information presented in this summary.

BASIC PRINCIPLES OF ECONOMICS

Most people's wants are unlimited. We can never be completely satisfied because the **limited resources** we have are not enough to satisfy our **unlimited wants**. For example, everyone in Grand Rapids may want a new home, but there is not enough space, materials, or money available to build such homes for everyone. Economists refer to the inability of *scarce* resources to meet our unlimited wants as the **problem of scarcity**.

Because of the problem of scarcity, every time we choose to satisfy one of our wants, we give up the chance to satisfy other wants. For example, if you use your money to buy a new stereo, you give up the opportunity to buy a computer. This trade-off — giving up the opportunity to satisfy other wants — is called the **opportunity cost** of an economic choice.

THE THREE BASIC ECONOMIC QUESTIONS

In deciding how to deal with the problem of scarcity, every society must answer three basic economic questions:

***What* should be produced?**

***How* should it be produced?**

***Who* should get what is produced?**

The Role of Economic Systems. How a society answers these three questions is known as its **economic system**. In some societies, the government decides the answers. In other societies, the answers are based on tradition and custom. Finally, in a free market system, producers and consumers decide by making their own choices.

CONSUMERS AND PRODUCERS IN A FREE MARKET ECONOMY

The United States has a **free market system**. In this type of system, producers and consumers act freely. Their actions determine what is made and who gets it.

A **producer** is a person or business that supplies goods and services. **Goods** are items that people make and use, like toys, food, and cars. **Services** are things that people do for others. For example, a doctor provides medical services. **Production** is the act of making or providing goods and services.

Production: A wooden shoe factory

Consumers are people and businesses that use goods and services to satisfy their needs and wants. For example, a consumer uses foods by eating them and uses clothes by wearing them. **Consumption** is the act of using goods and services.

Consumption: shoppers at an East Lansing Arts Festival

Profits. Producers make goods or provide services in order to make a **profit**. Producers sell to consumers at a **price** they think consumers are willing to pay. The difference between the producer's costs and the selling price is known as the profit. For example, if it costs $7 to make a T-shirt and the shirt sells for $13, the profit is $6.

Supply and Demand. The amount of goods and services that producers make is called the **supply**. The **demand** is the amount of items or services consumers are willing to buy. If many consumers want to buy a product, producers will make more of it because of the strong demand. If very few consumers want to buy a product, producers will stop making it. In this way, consumers are able to influence what is produced: they decide which products and services they want to buy and how much they are willing to pay for them. The interaction of producers and consumers also determines prices.

Buying on Credit. Consumers are influenced by how much money they have to spend. Individuals, businesses, and governments are sometimes able to borrow money to buy goods and services. The borrower pays **interest** for the money that is borrowed. This is known as **buying on credit**. Some of the most common ways to buy on credit are **installment buying** and **credit card purchases**.

Credit allows us to buy goods and services we could not otherwise afford. We can take advantage of special sales or investment opportunities, or meet sudden emergencies. However, the use of credit also has its costs and risks. We have to pay interest to the lender. This adds to the cost of purchases. In addition, when credit is too easy to get, people sometimes spend more than they can afford.

THE FACTORS OF PRODUCTION

Four **factors of production** are needed to produce goods and services:

1. NATURAL RESOURCES **Natural resources** are all the resources found in nature. These resources include minerals, trees, water, plants and soil.	**2. HUMAN CAPITAL** **Human capital** (also called **labor**) is the work that people do to make goods or to provide services. It includes the talents, training, skills and knowledge of the people who produce goods and provide services.
3. CAPITAL EQUIPMENT **Capital equipment** consists of things that are used to make other goods or to perform services. For example, machines and tools are capital equipment.	**4. ENTREPRENEURS (A form of human capital)** Natural resources, human capital, and capital equipment must be combined in order to make something. **Entrepreneurs** are people who combine them. They invest their money and are the owners of businesses.

FORMS OF BUSINESS ORGANIZATION

Businesses are formed to produce and sell goods and services in order to make a profit. Various forms of business organization help make it possible to bring together human capital, natural resources, and capital equipment in large amounts. In the United States, businesses can be organized in several ways.

- ✦ A **single ownership** is a business owned by one person or a family. The owner is personally liable *(responsible)* for the business and its debts.
- ✦ A **partnership** is a business with two or more owners who are jointly responsible for the business and its debts.
- ✦ A **corporation** is a form of business with a life of its own. Investors, called stockholders, buy shares in the company. They are not directly involved in running the corporation and are not personally liable for the company's debts.

HOW GOVERNMENT AFFECTS THE ECONOMY

Even in a free market system, the government has an important influence on the economy. The government prints money, collects taxes, and employs workers. The government acts like a police officer in the marketplace. It makes sure that people and businesses live by certain rules and treat each other fairly. Government also supplies citizens with some goods and services, such as public schools, parks, and roads. Goods and services provided by government are known as **public goods** and **public services**. They are paid for with the tax money government collects, or by government borrowing.

Road repair in Lansing, an example of a public service paid for by taxes

LEVELS OF GOVERNMENT AFFECTING THE ECONOMY

Federal Government prints money, collects national income taxes, and pays for our national defense, regulates Social Security, and sets minimum wages.	**State Government** collects state income taxes, and pays for state highways, state courts, and prisons. It also gives money to local schools around the state.	**Local Government** collects local sales taxes and property taxes, and pays for local schools, police, parks, and other services.

THE ECONOMY OF MICHIGAN

Michigan is an important part of the American economy. The location of the state has had a great influence on its economic development. Because Michigan is on the Great Lakes, people throughout the Midwest have sent goods up-river into the lakes and across to Michigan. Deposits of iron ore and copper in the Upper Peninsula also helped develop Michigan's industries. Because Michigan borders Canada, its has become a center for U.S.-Canadian trade.

THE ROLE OF INTERNATIONAL TRADE

The American economy forms part of a larger global economy. Because of improvements in communications and transportation, trade among countries has increased tremendously over the last hundred years. Almost every country in the world has become dependent on trading with other countries, leading to **global interdependence**. Particular countries often have special advantages that make it easier for them to produce some goods rather than others. For example, Japan may import coffee from Colombia. To **import** is to bring in goods from a foreign country. At the same time, Japan may export automobiles to Colombia. To **export** is to send goods to be sold in a foreign country.

SECTION 2

MAJOR ECONOMIC TERMS AND CONCEPTS

Use this graphic organizer to review your understanding of important economics terms and concepts.

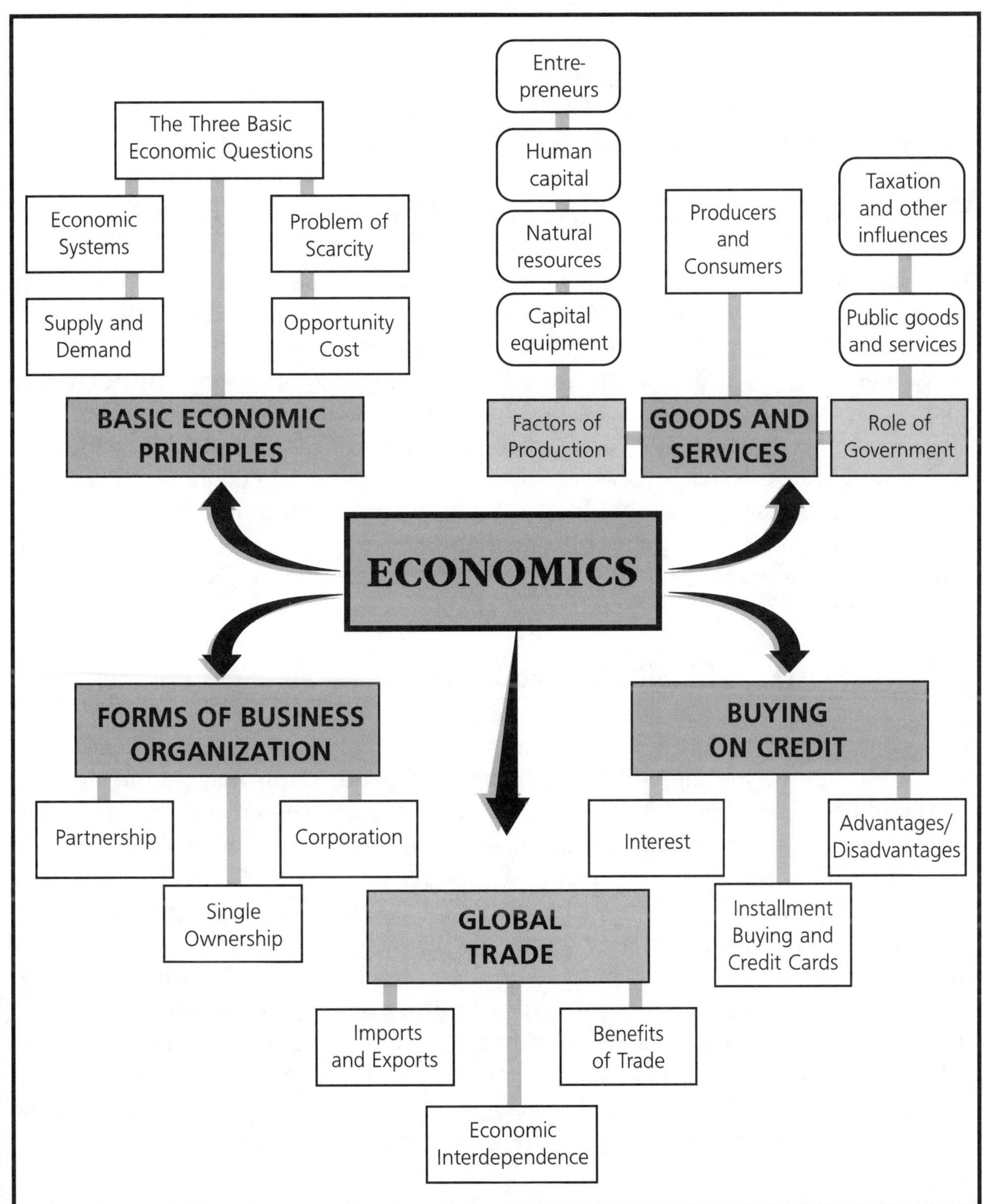

SECTION 3

THE "BIG IDEAS" IN ECONOMICS

Remember that prompts are used to test your understanding of the "big ideas." Therefore, you should understand what each standard requires for the test. The following section lists the "big ideas" for economics, grouped by standard.

STANDARD IV.1: INDIVIDUAL AND HOUSEHOLD CHOICES

This standard focuses on basic economic concepts and how they affect your daily economic choices. You should understand the concept of **scarcity** — that people have unlimited wants, but that a society can produce only a limited number of goods and services at any given time. You should also understand **opportunity cost** — that when we make an economic choice to satisfy a want, there is a trade-off: we give up the opportunity to satisfy other wants. This standard also requires you to weigh the advantages and disadvantages of a personal economic choice, and then make a decision. You should also know what **consumer credit** is, and the costs and benefits of using it. Lastly, you should know some alternatives to consumer credit, such as saving for a purchase in advance, working extra to pay for a purchase, or not making the purchase at all.

STANDARD IV.2: BUSINESS CHOICES

This standard focuses on how goods and services are produced in our economy. You should know the ingredients or **factors of production** that go into making goods and services. One factor of production is **natural resources** such as minerals, chemicals, and water. **Human capital** refers to the labor, management skills and knowledge that contribute to making a product or service. **Capital equipment** refers to the tools and machines, such as computers, that we use to produce goods and services. **Entrepreneurs** are business owners who invest their money and combine the other three factors of production. You are also required to know the main forms of business organization. An **individual owner** of a business is personally responsible for its debts. In a **partnership**, several people share in the profits and risks. Another way people pool their resources is by forming a **corporation**. The investors in a corporation are *not* personally responsible for the corporation's debts. The most they can lose is the money they have invested.

STANDARD IV.3: ROLE OF GOVERNMENT

This standard focuses on the role of government in the American economy. **Public goods** and **public services** are goods and services provided by the government and paid for by taxes. You should also understand that even in a **free market system** like ours, the government plays an important role in the economy. For example, the federal government manages the money supply, protects consumers and businesses from unfair practices, and provides a system of laws under which business can operate. Governments can also be major purchasers of goods and services. You should also be able to identify what particular ways each level of government may affect the economy. For example, your local government may affect the economy of your community by collecting a local sales tax, or by providing certain public goods and services.

STANDARD IV.4: ECONOMIC SYSTEMS

This standard focuses on how a free market economy works. You should be able to identify how supply and demand determine what goods and services are produced in a free market economy, and the **price** of these goods and services. **Producers** provide goods and services in order to make a **profit**. **Consumers** are willing to buy goods and services at a certain price to satisfy their needs and wants. The interaction of these forces determines what is produced and at what price it is sold. You should also understand that each of us acts as a producer through our work and acts as a consumer when we buy and use goods and services. Finally, you should be able to explain how Michigan's abundant natural resources and location on the Great Lakes (next to Canada, and across from the Erie Canal) have affected its economic growth.

STANDARD IV.5: TRADE

This standard looks at the role of international trade in our interdependent world. You should understand how the United States acts as a part of a global economy. You should be able to identify common household items that come from other countries. You should also understand that particular countries sometimes have special advantages that makes it cheaper and more efficient for them to produce certain goods. For example, your household may have coffee grown in Brazil or cotton shirts made in China. Finally, this standard requires you to know something about how international trade works. **Exporters** ship goods to other countries. **Importers** bring goods into their country and often pay special taxes on these goods, known as **customs duties**. For example, many Canadian goods are imported into the United States through Michigan.

PRACTICE QUESTIONS

— SELECTED-RESPONSE QUESTIONS —

These questions contain two prompts with five questions for each prompt. Examine each prompt carefully and then answer the questions that follow it. Each question has a corresponding benchmark to show you which "big idea" is being tested. A list of the benchmarks for economics can be found at the end of this chapter.

Directions: Study the following information and table and use them with what you already know to answer the questions that follow.

John earns $10 a week for doing chores around the house. He decided to put together a simple budget for the next five weeks.

JOHN'S BUDGET

CHOICES	COST
1. Candy	$9
2. Movies	$16
3. Clothes	$25

1 By putting together a budget, John recognized the economic concept of

A scarcity
B interdependence
C factors of production
D forms of business organization

IV.1.LE.1

2 When John spends the money he has budgeted to buy candy, he is acting as

A a producer
B a consumer
C an exporter
D an entrepreneur

IV.4.LE.2

3 If John decides to spend movie money to buy clothes, the fact that he can no longer use that money to go to the movies is referred to as

A scarcity
B a natural resource
C a public good
D an opportunity cost

IV.1.LE.2

4 What event would BEST explain a rise in the price of Choice 1?

A A plant disease destroys much of the world's supply of sugar cane.
B Exports of chocolate to the United States increase.
C The national government cuts taxes on all candy manufacturers.
D Michigan builds a new highway system across the state.

IV.4.LE.1

5 What would be a DISADVANTAGE of John's using a credit card to buy all three choices if he did not have enough money to pay for them?

A He could buy the items when they are on sale.
B He would have to pay interest on the credit card debt.
C He would not have to wait until he had the money available.
D He would have to pay more tax.

IV.1.LE.4

Name ______________________ Teacher ______________________

Directions: Study the following diagram. Use it with what you already know to answer the questions that follow.

A. NATURAL RESOURCES

C. CAPITAL EQUIPMENT

A house being built

B. HUMAN CAPITAL

D. ENTREPRENEURSHIP

6 The four items listed in the boxes are referred to as

A public goods
B the factors of production
C the problem of scarcity
D opportunity cost

IV.2.LE.1

7 What item might correctly be included in the category in BOX C?

A water
B partnership
C plumber
D electric drills

IV.2.LE.1

8 Which of the following would likely cause an increase in the price of the house?

A the price of lumber goes down
B land prices decrease
C there is a shortage of workers available to build houses
D the cost of builders' tools goes down

IV.3.LE.2

9 If a person were to build a house like the one in the picture for the purpose of selling it, that person would be acting as a

A producer
B consumer
C exporter
D importer

IV.5.LE.2

10 What would be included in BOX B?

A hammers
B nails
C lumber
D carpenters

IV.4.LE.1

Name ______________________ Teacher ______________________

— CONSTRUCTED-RESPONSE QUESTIONS —

The following section has two constructed-response questions. Read the directions and examine each question carefully before answering. Each question has a corresponding benchmark number to show you which "big idea" is being tested.

Directions: You should take about 5 minutes to read the following material and use it with what you already know to complete this task.

11 Many times in your life you have had to decide what to buy from a choice of two or more items. On the lines provided, identify a situation in which you faced the problem of scarcity. Identify your choice, and explain the opportunity cost of your decision.

Identify a choice you faced because the problem of scarcity:

____

____

____

IV.1.LE.1

Explain the opportunity cost of your decision:

____

____

____

____

____

____

IV.1.LE.2

Name ______________________ Teacher ______________________

Directions: You should take about 5 minutes to read the following and use it with what you already know to complete this task.

Dear Uncle Ted,

I saw this diagram in a newspaper article about the importance of world trade. However, I still do not understand how world trade affects me.

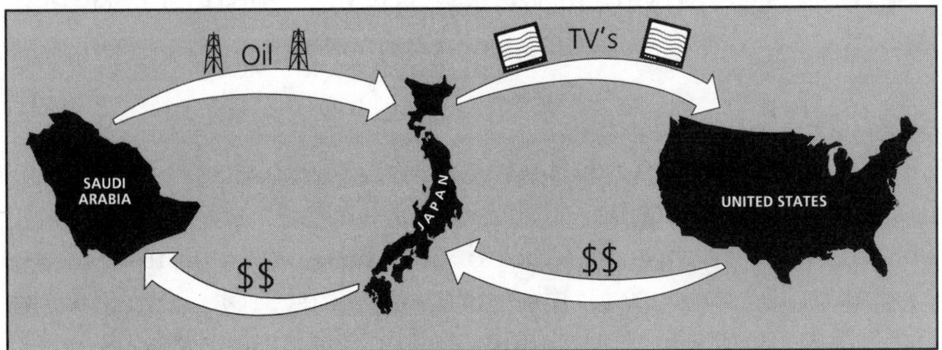

Since your business is importing TV sets, Mom suggested I write you for an explanation of how international trade affects me and other people in Michigan.

Your niece,
Nancy

11 On the line provided, identify a good or service that Japan sells to the United States. Then complete the letter of reply. IV.5.LE.1

Identification of a good or service Japan sells to the United States. ____________

Dear Nancy,

I was happy to receive your letter. I would very much like to answer your question. Trade affects the people of Michigan in many ways. For example,

____

____

____

____

____

____

IV.5.LE.2

Name ____________________ Teacher ____________________

BENCHMARKS OF THE ECONOMICS STRAND

Standard IV.1: Individual and Household Choices

IV.1.LE.1 Explain why people must face scarcity when making economic decisions.

IV.1.LE.2 Identify the opportunity costs in personal decision-making situations.

IV.1.LE.3 Use a decision-making model to explain a personal choice.

IV.1.LE.4 Analyze the costs, benefits, and alternatives to using consumer credit.

Standard IV.2: Business Choices

IV.2.LE.1 Distinguish between natural resources, human capital, and capital equipment in the production of a good or service.

IV.2.LE.2 Distinguish among individual ownership, partnership and corporation.

IV.2.LE.3 Examine the historical and contemporary role a major industry has played in the state of Michigan and in the United States.

Standard IV.3: Role of Government

IV.3.LE.1 Use a decision-making model to explain a choice involving a public good or service.

IV.3.LE.2 Distinguish between the economic roles of local, state, and federal governments and cite examples of each.

IV.3.LE.3 Use a local example to assess the effectiveness of the government at providing public goods or resolving an economic dispute.

Standard IV.4: Economic Systems

IV.4.LE.1 Explain how prices are determined in a market economy and how they serve as a means of allocating resources.

IV.4.LE.2 Describe how they act as a producer and a consumer.

IV.4.LE.3 Analyze how Michigan's location has impacted its economic development.

Standard IV.5: Trade

IV.5.LE.1 Trace the national origin of common household items and the trade flows which brought them to the United States.

IV.5.LE.1 Describe benefits of international trade to consumers and producers.

IV.5.LE.1 Describe how businesses are involved in trade as producers, distributors, importers, and exporters.

CHAPTER 8

CIVICS

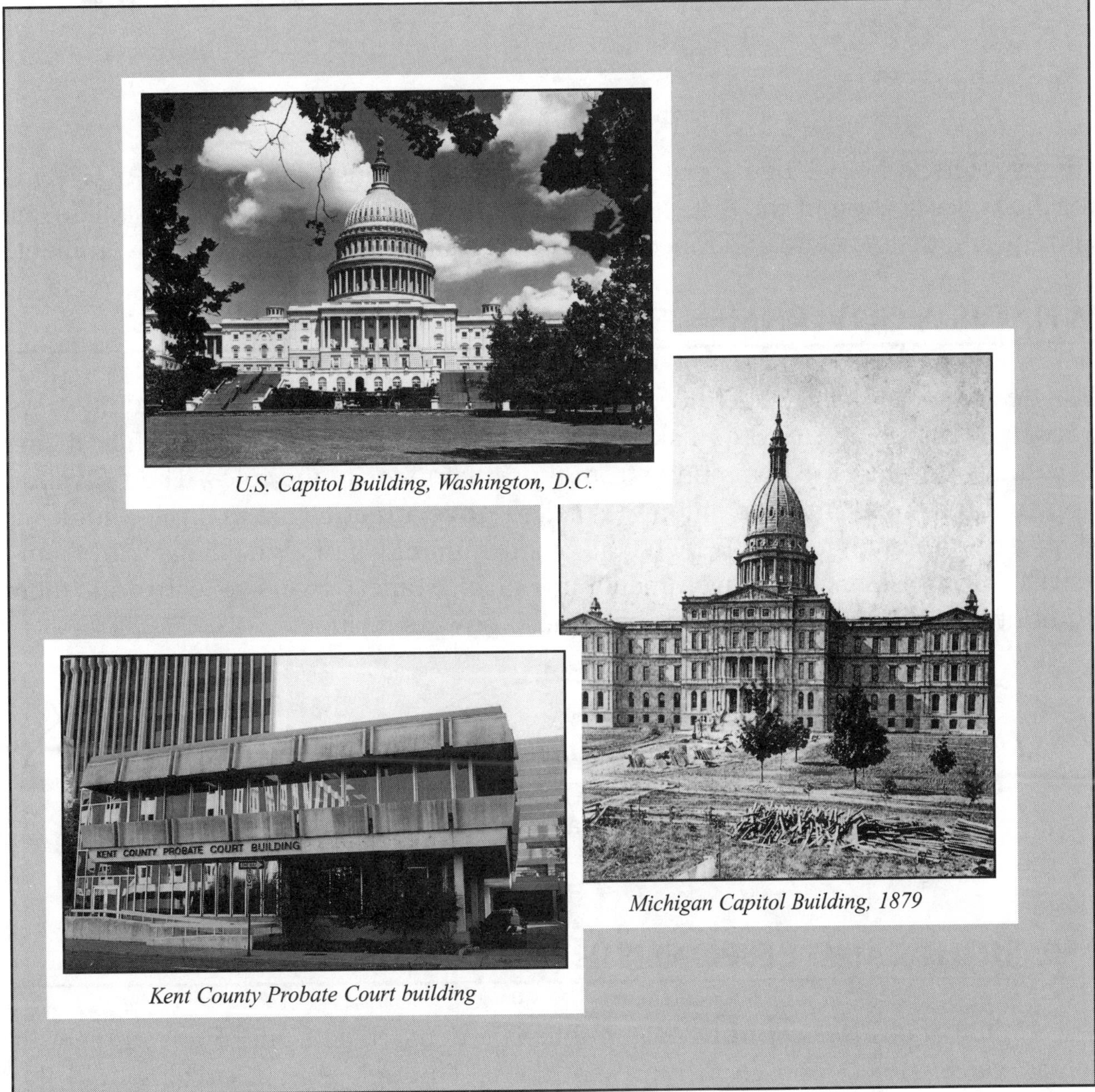

U.S. Capitol Building, Washington, D.C.

Michigan Capitol Building, 1879

Kent County Probate Court building

A CAPSULE SUMMARY OF CIVICS

Civics refers to knowledge about government that citizens should have. To prepare for the civics section of the test, you should review the rights and responsibilities of citizens and the structure and functions of your local, state, and national government.

WHAT IS A GOVERNMENT?

People are social beings: they need to live with others in groups or communities. As a result, communities need to make rules to settle disagreements among their members and to protect the community from those who violate the rules. The organization set up to protect the community is called **government**. Just as a pilot guides a ship, a government guides the members of a community in their dealings with themselves and outsiders. All governments are given some powers to carry out their authority over the members of society. These powers include:

a *legislative* power to make the laws

an *executive* power to carry out the laws

a *judicial* power to interpret the laws

THE RIGHTS AND RESPONSIBILITIES OF AMERICAN CITIZENS

The United States is a **republic**. A republic is a democratic form of government in which citizens elect people to represent them. Through voting, citizens hold the final power over government. Americans have basic **rights** such as freedom of speech, freedom of the press, and freedom of religion. This ensures that while the **majority rules**, **minority rights** are also protected. American citizens also have important **responsibilities**, such as becoming informed on important issues, and voting in elections. The success of a democratic form of government depends on citizens fulfilling their responsibilities as well as protecting their rights and the rights of others.

GOALS OF THE UNITED STATES GOVERNMENT

The goals of our national government are stated in two important documents: the Declaration of Independence and the U.S. Constitution.

- **Declaration of Independence**. The Declaration of Independence states that the main goal of government should be to protect the rights of citizens, especially their rights to "life, liberty and the pursuit of happiness."

The signing of the Declaration of Independence

- **U.S. Constitution**. A **constitution** is a written plan of government. The founders of our government struck a balance between the powers of government and the rights of the individual. The **Preamble** to the U.S. Constitution states the goals and purposes of our national government — to promote peace, provide for the nation's defense, establish justice, protect rights, and promote the general well-being. The first ten amendments to the Constitution, known as the **Bill of Rights**, guarantee individual rights such as freedom of speech.

THE ORGANIZATION OF THE UNITED STATES GOVERNMENT

The organization of our national government was established in the Constitution. Under the Constitution, the powers of our government are limited. Government authorities can take only those actions specifically permitted by the Constitution. The Constitution also created a system in which power was shared between the national government and the state governments. This division of powers is called **federalism**. The national (federal) government deals with matters that affect the whole country, as well as relations between the states. The state governments handle matters within each state. In both the national and state governments, power was further divided among three branches: the legislative, executive, and judicial.

THE NATIONAL GOVERNMENT

LEGISLATIVE BRANCH
(makes laws for the nation)

Congress of the United States

U.S. House of Representatives

- Members are elected for 2-year terms
- States are represented according to the size of their population

U.S. Senate

- Members are elected for 6-year terms
- Each state has two Senators

EXECUTIVE BRANCH
(carries out national laws)

President of the United States

Elected for a 4-year term

- Commander-in-Chief of the armed forces
- Proposes national budget
- Enforces laws passed by Congress
- Can veto (reject) bills passed by Congress

JUDICIAL BRANCH
(interprets national laws)

United States Supreme Court

- Justices are appointed for life terms

Other National Courts

- Justices are appointed for life terms

MICHIGAN STATE GOVERNMENT

Like our national government, Michigan's state government also has three branches which make, enforce, and interpret the laws.

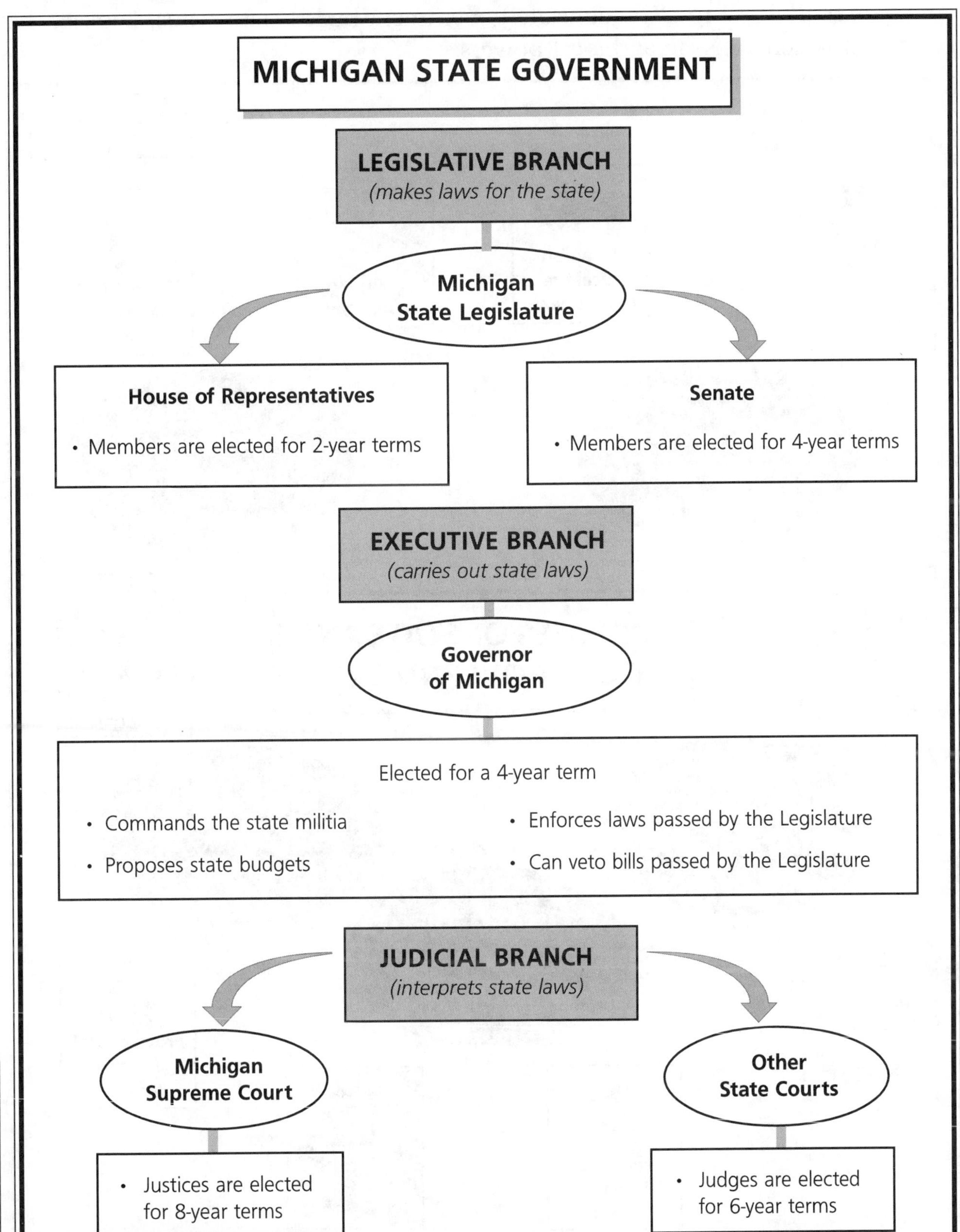

MICHIGAN STATE GOVERNMENT
LEGISLATIVE BRANCH
(makes laws for the state)
Michigan State Legislature
House of Representatives
• Members are elected for 2-year terms
Senate
• Members are elected for 4-year terms
EXECUTIVE BRANCH
(carries out state laws)
Governor of Michigan
Elected for a 4-year term
• Commands the state militia
• Proposes state budgets
• Enforces laws passed by the Legislature
• Can veto bills passed by the Legislature
JUDICIAL BRANCH
(interprets state laws)
Michigan Supreme Court
• Justices are elected for 8-year terms
Other State Courts
• Judges are elected for 6-year terms

LOCAL GOVERNMENTS IN MICHIGAN

Under the state government are local governments such as county and town governments. State and local governments often have similar tasks; for example, town governments build local roads while state government builds state roads. Look at the key to tell which are state and local powers:

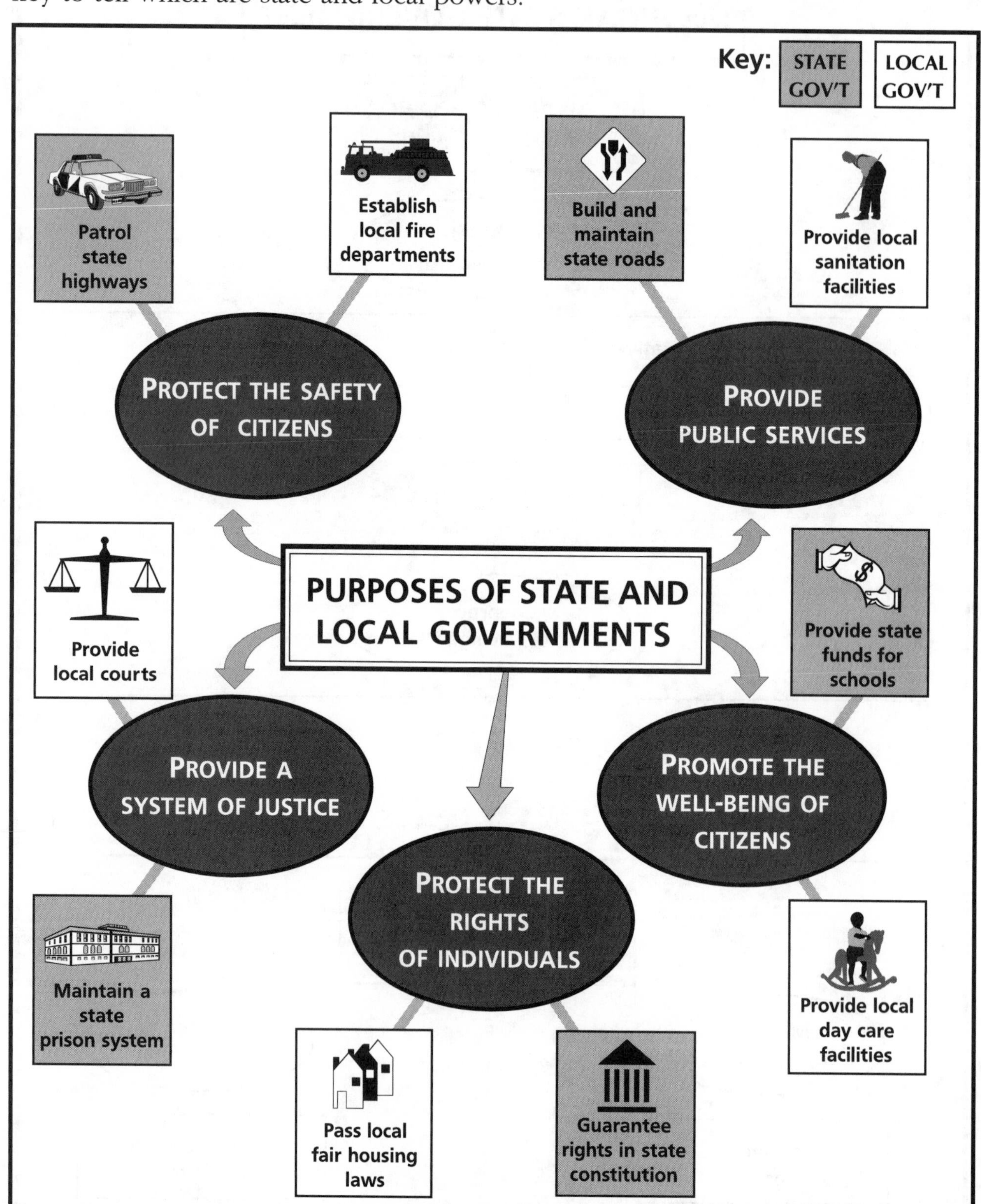

SECTION 2

MAJOR CIVICS TERMS AND CONCEPTS

Use the following graphic organizer as a review to see if you can recall these important terms and concepts in civics.

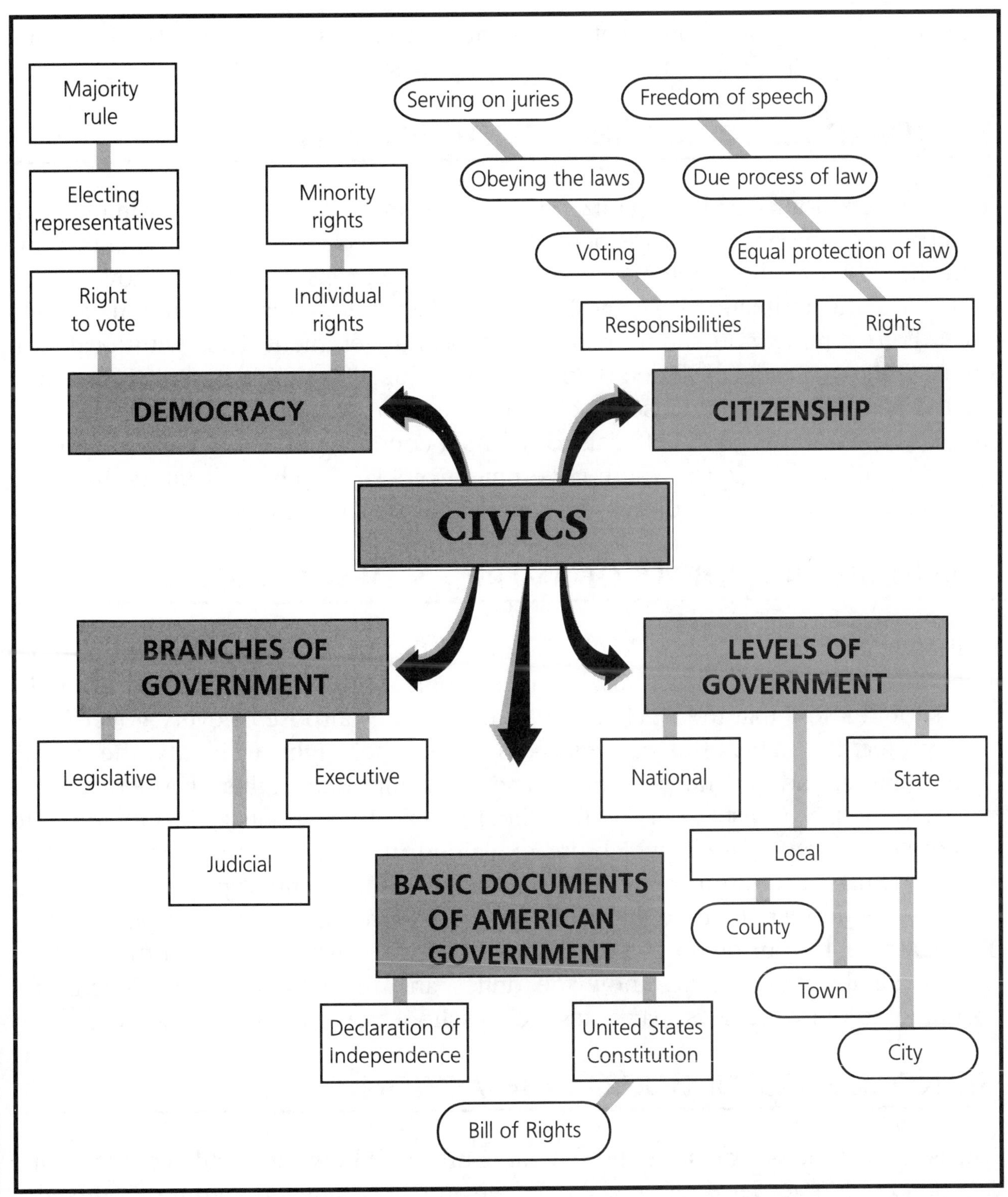

SECTION 3

THE "BIG IDEAS" IN CIVICS

It important for you to know what each standard requires for the test. The following sections list the "big ideas" for civics, grouped by standard.

STANDARD III.1: PURPOSES OF GOVERNMENT

This standard looks at the organization and power of American government. Our government can only do what is permitted by the Constitution and stated in the law. You should know the differences between the three levels of American government — local, state, and national — and be able to describe the main institutions at each level. For example, you should realize that local government deals with local concerns, while our national (federal) government deals with problems facing the entire United States. You should also be able to give examples of what our Constitution and laws permit our public officials to do. As a contrast, you should also be able to give examples of societies where government officials, such as dictators, have the power to act without the consent of their citizens or authority of law.

STANDARD III.2: IDEALS OF AMERICAN DEMOCRACY

This standard requires you to know the events that led to the Declaration of Independence. You also need to know the main points of the Declaration. For example, you should know that the Declaration states that the purpose of every government is to protect the rights of its citizens — especially their rights to liberty, the pursuit of happiness, and general prosperity. The most important rights of Americans are found in the U.S. Constitution and the Bill of Rights. These rights are also referred to as *core democratic values*, which are explained in Chapter 10 of this book. Test questions may ask you to name some of these rights, or might present a situation and ask you to identify the right that is involved. Rights also require responsibilities. For example, for our own rights to be protected, we must also respect the rights of others. Finally, you should know the duties and responsibilities of citizens: for example, to obey the laws, pay taxes, go to school, serve on juries, and vote.

STANDARD III.3: DEMOCRACY IN ACTION

This standard focuses on state and federal courts, and how they settle conflicts. One job of a court is to decide if an accused person has committed a crime. Courts also settle disputes between two or more parties in a civil case. **Michigan state courts** handle disagreements between Michiganders or crimes involving Michigan's laws. **Federal courts** settle disputes between citizens of different states, or matters concerning federal law. Constitutional issues often arise in defining a right or when there is a conflict between different constitutional rights. For example, the Constitution guarantees our freedom of speech. However, does this give us the right to scream "Fire!" in a crowded movie theater as a joke? People might panic and be injured while trying to escape. Such constitutional issues are often settled by our highest federal court — the U.S. Supreme Court.

The room where the U.S. Supreme Court decides issues of federal law and constitutional rights

STANDARD III.4: AMERICAN GOVERNMENT AND POLITICS

This standard focuses on the organization of American government and how our political system works. You should know the three powers of government: making laws, enforcing laws, and interpreting laws. You should also understand that local, state, and federal governments are organized into three branches: legislative, executive, and judicial. You should be able to describe the duties of each branch at each level. You should also understand that different groups in society sometimes have conflicts. Laws provide a framework in which people can peacefully work out their differences. You should know what an election campaign is and be able to describe how citizens participate in one. For example, citizens can speak to friends on behalf of a candidate, pass around leaflets, attend election rallies, listen to election speeches, make campaign contributions, and vote for a candidate on election day.

STANDARD III.5: AMERICAN GOVERNMENT AND WORLD AFFAIRS

This standard concerns world affairs. You should be able to explain how different nations affect each other. You should also be able to give examples of events in other countries that have had an impact on Americans. For example, Iraq's invasion of Kuwait affected Americans by making oil prices higher. Finally, you should be able to show how events in the United States often affect people in other countries. For example, the development of American computers and software has greatly improved the sharing of medical, environmental, and other kinds of information around the world.

SECTION 4

PRACTICE QUESTIONS

— SELECTED-RESPONSE QUESTIONS —

Each of the following selected-response questions contains a prompt and five questions. Each question has a corresponding benchmark to show you what "big idea" is being tested. A list of the civics benchmarks is at the end of this chapter.

Directions: Study the following diagram and use it with what you already know to answer the questions that follow.

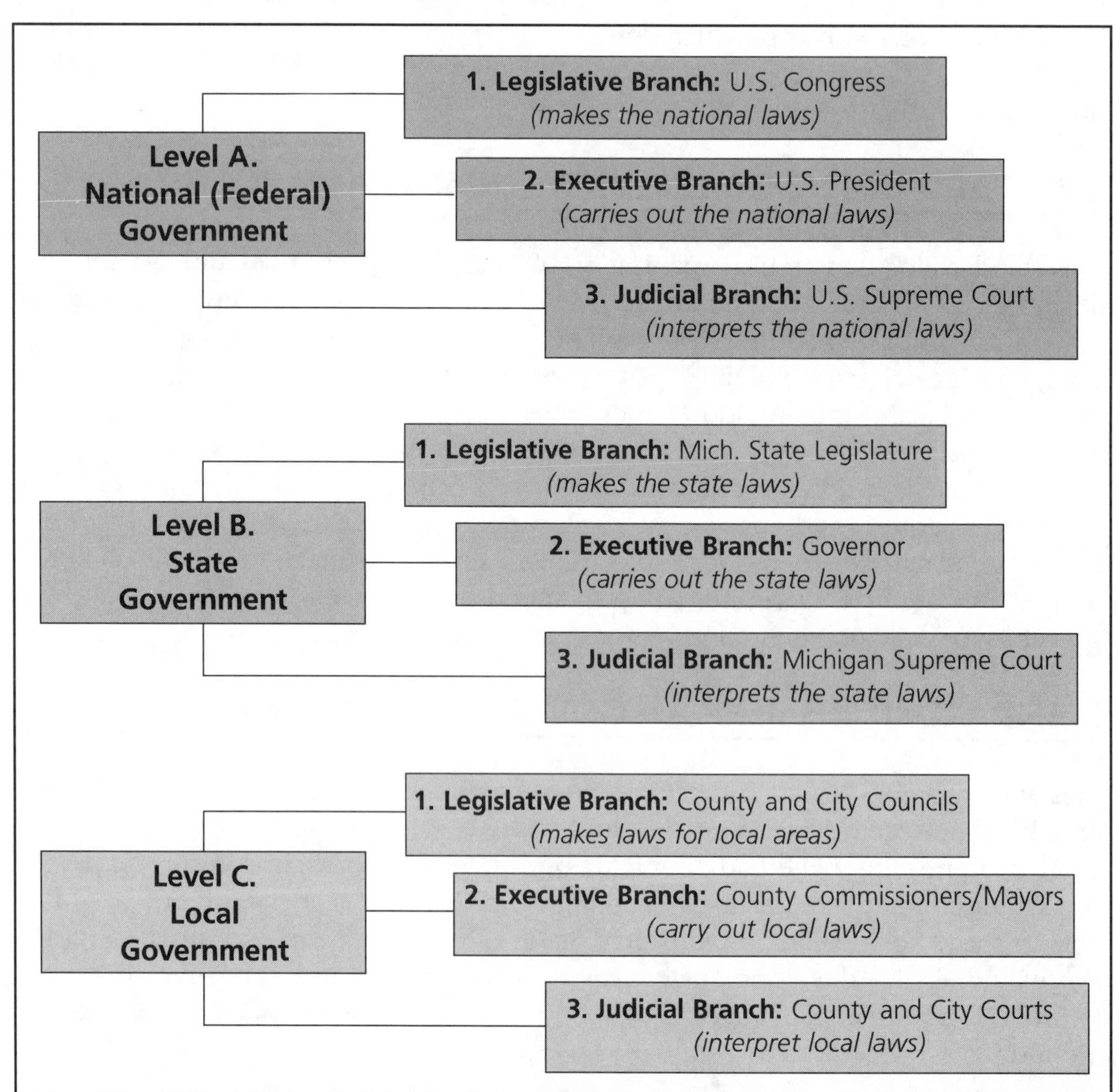

1 Which level and branch of government shown in the diagram would MOST likely be responsible for regulating trade with Canada?

A A-2
B B-3
C C-1
D C-3

III.1.LE.1

2 Which level and branch of government would be responsible for passing a law against dumping garbage on local roads?

A A-3
B B-1
C B-2
D C-1

III.1.LE.1

3 A County Commissioner handles the spending of tax money. Which level and branch of government does the Commissioner work in?

A A-1
B B-2
C A-3
D C-2

III.1.LE.2

4 Which level and branch of government would be responsible for submitting a budget to the State Legislature in Michigan?

A A-1
B B-2
C C-1
D A-2

III.4.LE.3

5 Which level and branch of government would MOST likely deal with deciding if the U.S. Constitution has been violated?

A A-2
B B-2
C A-3
D C-2

III.4.LE.2

Name ______________________ Teacher ______________________

Directions: Study the following reading passage. Use it with what you already know to answer the questions that follow.

The U. S. Constitution was approved only after its supporters promised a future "Bill of Rights." To protect individuals from abuses by the national government, the **Bill of Rights** — the first ten amendments to the Constitution — was adopted in 1791. Since then, 17 other amendments have been added. Many of the amendments guarantee rights that cannot be taken away by the government. These rights generally fall into four groups:

GROUP 1: FREEDOM OF EXPRESSION

These rights protect our freedom to express our opinions. The First Amendment guarantees our freedom of speech. However, there are limits to what people can say in public places. For example, a person cannot say things that will cause a riot or some other disturbance that endangers innocent people.

GROUP 2: DUE PROCESS RIGHTS

"Due process" means that the government must follow specific procedures when it accuses a person of a crime or takes away someone's property for the public good. The government cannot use unfair methods. For example, government officials must have a reasonable cause for suspicion before they can search someone's property.

GROUP 3: EQUAL PROTECTION

Other constitutional amendments guarantee "equal protection of the law" to all citizens. This means that every citizen will be treated equally by any law that is made by federal, state, or local government.

GROUP 4: VOTING RIGHTS

American citizens cannot be denied the right to vote based on their race, religion, nationality, or gender.

6 Based on the passage, which BEST explains why the Bill of Rights was added to the U.S. Constitution?

A The states wanted to limit individual rights.
B Some people feared government abuses.
C People wanted to divide government power between the states and the nation.
D The U.S. Congress wanted to protect its power.

III.2.LE.2

7 A person jokingly shouts "Fire!" in a crowded theater. According to the passage, is this action protected by the Bill of Rights?

A No, people cannot use Group 1 rights to put others in immediate danger without a good reason.
B Yes, that person is exercising the right to free speech.
C No, shouting in crowded public theaters is always against the law.
D Yes, the right of free assembly protects this person.

III.2.LE.2

8 The police in your town are stopping and searching all teenagers for illegal drugs, even when they don't look suspicious. Is this action allowed under the Constitution?

A No, because the police must respect the teens' Group 2 rights.
B No, because the police must always ask for permission to search someone.
C No, because of the teens' Group 1 rights.
D Yes, because the police have the right to search anyone whenever they want.

III.2.LE.2

9 Your high school's bowling team allows only girls to join. According to the passage, is this likely to be permitted by the Constitution?

A Yes, because this protects the girls' Group 1 rights.
B No, because this violates the boys' Group 1 rights.
C Yes, because the majority of the girls in the school voted to keep boys off the team.
D No, because this violates the boys' Group 3 rights.

III.2.LE.2

10 Putting a person on trial for murder without a jury would be a violation of the person's rights in

A Group 1
B Group 2
C Group 3
D Group 4

III.2.LE.2

Name ______________________ Teacher ______________________

— CONSTRUCTED-RESPONSE QUESTIONS —

The following section has two constructed-response questions. Read the directions and examine each question carefully before answering. Each question has a corresponding benchmark to show you what "big idea" is being tested.

Directions: You should take about 5 minutes to read the following material and use it with what you already know to complete this task.

Paris, France

Dear Michael,

From your letter I was surprised to learn that the Michigan Board of Education makes rules for your schools. Here in France, public schools are controlled by the Ministry of National Education. It sets up all requirements and decides what students throughout France will study.

Our teacher has told us that things are done differently in America. Since you're my pen pal, could you explain the three "levels of government" in your country? I'd also like to know what kinds of things the different levels of government in the United States do.

Your friend,
Dominique

11 Identify which level of government is responsible for deciding what subjects Michigan students will study in school:

____

On the lines provided, identify two other levels of government and one responsibility that each level has.

One level of government: ______________________

One responsibility it has: ____________________________________

____

Another level of government: ____________________

One responsibility it has: ____________________________________

____

III.1.LE.1

Name __________________________ Teacher __________________________

Directions: You should take about 5 minutes to read the following material and use it with what you already know to complete this task.

12 All U.S. citizens have certain basic rights. They also have responsibilities. A right is something that every citizen is allowed to do. Responsibilities, on the other hand, are the "shoulds" of citizenship — what good citizens are expected to do.

On the lines provided, identify *one right* we have and explain how it protects us from abuses of power by government. Then identify *one responsibility* we have, and explain how that responsibility helps make our government work more effectively.

Identification of a right: ______________________________

How this right protects us from abuses of power by government:

____

____

____

____

______________________________ III.2.LE.2

Identification of a responsibility:______________________________

How our fulfilling this responsibility makes government more effective:

____

____

____

____

______________________________ III.2.LE.3

Name ______________________ Teacher ______________________

BENCHMARKS FOR THE CIVICS STRAND

Standard III.1: Purposes of Government

III.1.LE.1 Distinguish among local, state and national government in the U.S. and describe the roles of government institutions at all three levels.

III.1.LE .2 Give examples of authority and the use of power without authority.

III.1.LE .3 Give reasons for limiting the power of government.

Standard III.2: Ideals of American Democracy

III.2.LE .1 Interpret the development and summarize the main points in the Declaration Independence.

III.2.LE .2 Interpret the meaning of specific rights guaranteed by the Constitution including religious liberty, free expression, privacy, property, due process of law and equal protection of the law.

III.2.LE.3 Explain responsibilities citizens have to uphold constitutional rights.

Standard III.3: Democracy In Action

III.3.LE.1 Describe what state and federal courts are expected to do.

III.3.LE.2 Describe issues that arise over constitutional issues.

Standard III.4: American Government and Politics

III.4.LE.1 Distinguish among making, enforcing and interpreting laws.

III.4.LE.2 Explain how law is used to manage conflict in American society.

III.4.LE.3 Explain the basic organization of the local, state and federal governments.

III.4.LE.4 Describe how citizens participate in election campaigns.

Standard III.5: American Government and World Affairs

III.5.LE.1 Explain various ways that nations of the world interact with each other.

III.5.LE.2 Describe events in other countries that have affected Americans and, conversely, events within the U.S. that have affected other countries.

CHAPTER 9

INQUIRY

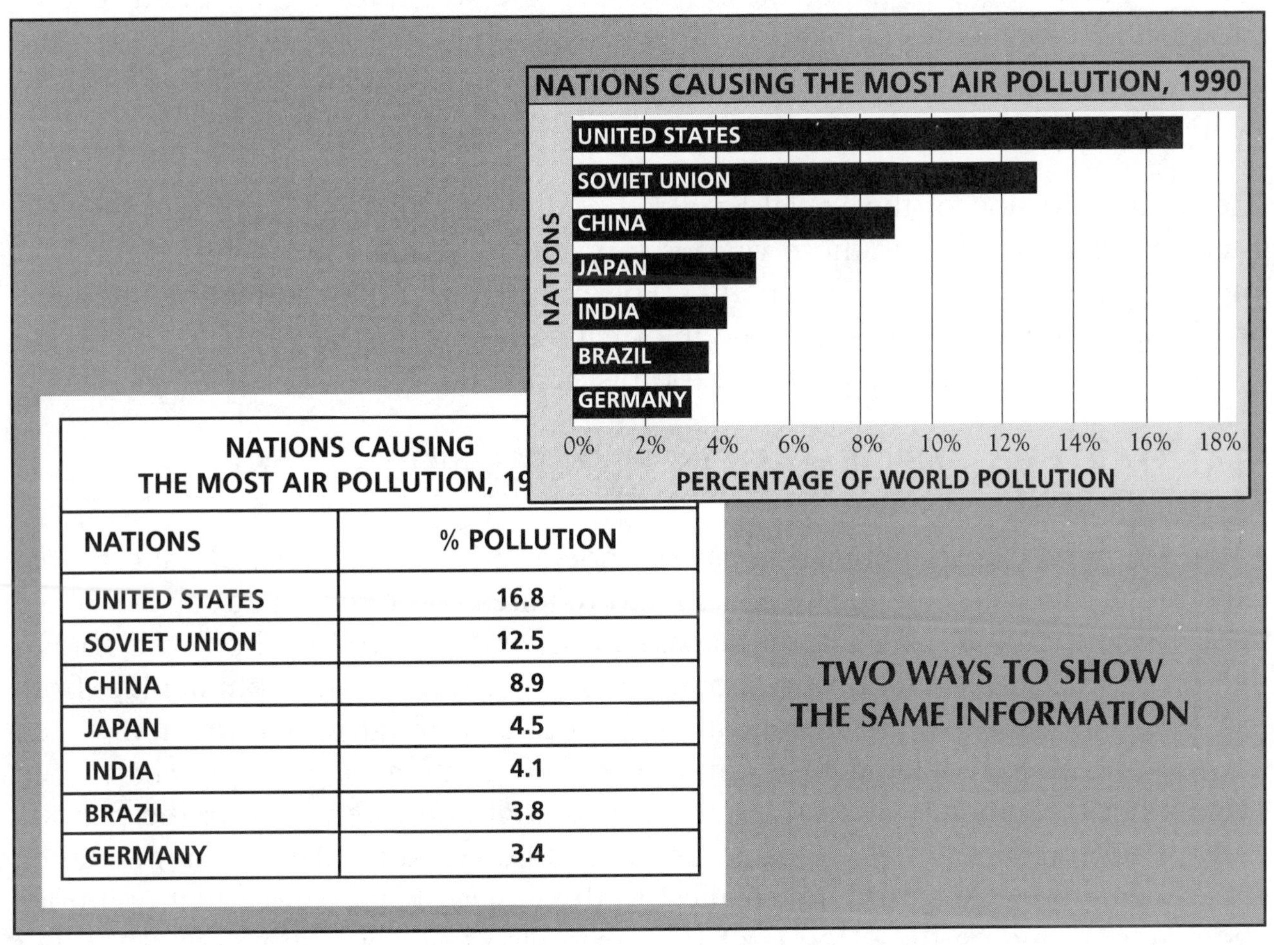

NATIONS CAUSING THE MOST AIR POLLUTION, 19

NATIONS	% POLLUTION
UNITED STATES	16.8
SOVIET UNION	12.5
CHINA	8.9
JAPAN	4.5
INDIA	4.1
BRAZIL	3.8
GERMANY	3.4

INQUIRY BENCHMARKS

One of the main purposes of social studies is to help prepare young people to become responsible citizens. A responsible citizen must be able to participate in public discussions of important issues. In order to participate effectively, a person must be knowledgeable about these issues. In the world today, we often receive information about issues in a variety of formats, such as line graphs, bar graphs, pie charts, tables, timelines, and maps. These formats have already been described in Chapter 2 of this book.

The inquiry section of the Social Studies MEAP Test will examine your ability to interpret information from these various formats, as well as your ability to convert information from one format to another. For example, you may be required to interpret a bar graph and to re-format the information it contains into a table. Following are the "big ideas" that will be tested for this standard.

STANDARD V.1: INFORMATION PROCESSING

Social scientists examine human behavior and societies to find general patterns that explain why we act as we do. This standard requires you to organize social science information to make and interpret maps, graphs, and tables. You should be able to interpret social science information about local, state, and national communities from maps, graphs, and charts. This standard also requires you to take information, which may be presented in a table or list, and to convert it into a map, graph, chart, or in some other meaningful way. For example, you might be given a list of the populations of several states in alphabetical order, and be asked to place them in a table, reorganizing the states from the smallest to the largest. Finally, note that questions about understanding these forms of data may also test your knowledge of other strands at the same time.

SECTION 2 EXAMINING AN INQUIRY QUESTION

Now that you are familiar with what the inquiry strand focuses on, let's look at a typical inquiry question:

Directions: You should take about five minutes to study the following material and use it with what you already know to complete these tasks.

POPULATION OF THE FOUR LARGEST CITIES ON THE LOWER PENINSULA OF MICHIGAN (1990)

CITY	POPULATION
Detroit	1,027,974
Grand Rapids	189,000
Warren	145,000
Flint	141,000

POPULATION OF THE FOUR LARGEST CITIES ON THE UPPER PENINSULA OF MICHIGAN (1990)

CITY	POPULATION
Marquette	21,000
Sault Ste. Marie	14,689
Menominee	9,398
Iron Mountain	8,525

Task I

Based on the information in the tables, which of the following statements BEST describes the relationship between **population size** and the **location of cities** in Michigan?

A The northern part of the Lower Peninsula has the largest cities.

B The cities with the largest populations are located in the Lower Peninsula.

C Most large cities are in the western part of Michigan.

D Most of Michigan's large cities border Lake Michigan.

continued ...

TASK II
Use the information in the tables.

- Select **two cities** on the Lower Peninsula and write their names on the map of Michigan below, close to their proper locations. Choose the appropriate symbol from the legend, and draw it next to the name of each city.

- Select **one city** on the Upper Peninsula and write it on the map, close to its proper location. Draw the appropriate symbol from the legend next to the name of the city.

Legend:

 City with more than 100,000 people

 City with less than 25,000 people

A careful examination of the question shows that there are three parts for you to deal with:

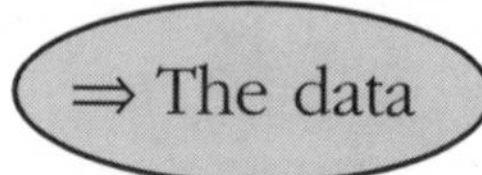

Let's look at each one separately, to see what is required in presenting an answer.

THE DATA

An inquiry question will always present you with some information, usually about a general topic. In the data presented, there will be **two** things (called *variables*) that deal with the general topic. In our sample question, the general topic and the two variables are as follows:

General Topic:	Cities in Michigan
Variable #1:	Size of population
Variable #2:	Location (Upper or Lower)

TASK I: In Task I, you are asked to make a **connection** or to identify a **relationship** between the two variables by answering a selected-response question. What the question really tests is your ability to see common patterns. You have to look at the specific information with the purpose of finding a common pattern, general connection, or generalization. *(A complete explanation of generalizations can be found in* ***Michigan, Its Land and Its People****, on page 186.)*

In the tables on page 101 you can see that the four cities with the largest populations in Michigan, such as Detroit and Grand Rapids, are located in the Lower Peninsula. The largest cities of the Upper Peninsula, such as Marquette and Sault Ste. Marie, generally have smaller populations. This question tests your ability to interpret social science information about local, state, and national communities from maps, graphs, and charts.

TASK II: In Task II, you will always be asked to take the information in the data and to **reorganize** it into **another type of data format**. For example, you may be given map information and be asked to put it into a table format. What the question really tests is your knowledge of data formats *(prompts)*. You have to know how the different formats are constructed. Chapter 2, you will recall, has a detailed description of each type of format.

In our sample question, you had to take information from the tables and transfer it onto the map. In order to do this, you had to know what a legend is. You also had to apply your knowledge of where major cities of Michigan are located. This question tested your ability to organize social science information to make and interpret maps, graphs, and tables.

On the following page is a sample answer to Task II.

Marquette

Grand Rapids

Detroit

City with more than 100,000 people

City with less than 25,000 people

A SAMPLE INQUIRY QUESTION

Directions: You should take about five minutes to study the following material and use it with what you already know to complete these tasks.

EDUCATION AND INCOME

Economists are often concerned with the high cost of education. They are especially interested in finding out whether a good education makes a person more productive in adult life.

continued ...

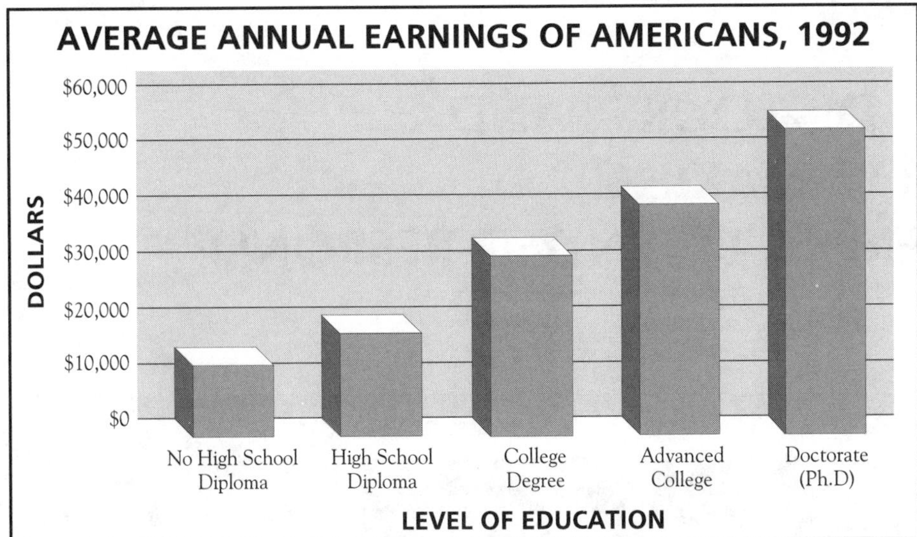

TASK I

Based on the information in the graph, which of the following statements BEST describes the relationship between **education** and **income**?

A Individuals with professional degrees always have higher incomes than those who have only completed college.

B Individuals with less education tend to have higher incomes than those with more education.

C Individuals with more education tend to have higher incomes than those with less education.

D Individuals without college degrees cannot make more than $20,000 a year.

TASK II

Organize the information into a table according to the amount of education *from lowest to highest.* Write each level of education and the average yearly earnings of people with that level in the correct locations on the table below.

AVERAGE EARNINGS BASED ON LEVEL OF EDUCATION

Level of Education	Average Annual Earnings (1992)
1.	
2.	
3.	
4.	
5.	

Name________________________________ Teacher________________________________

CHAPTER 10

PUBLIC DISCOURSE AND DECISION-MAKING: ANSWERING EXTENDED-RESPONSE QUESTIONS

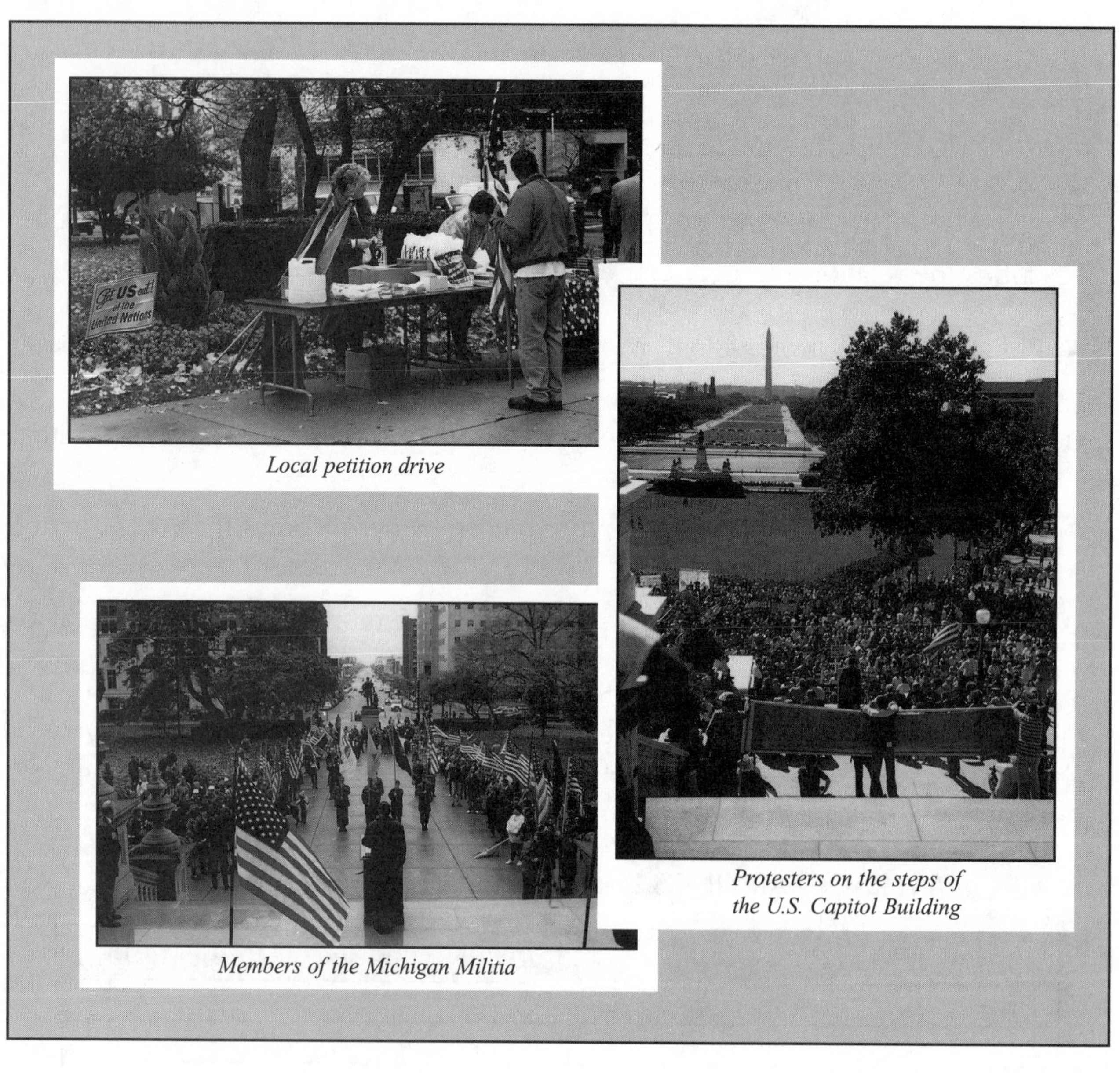

Local petition drive

Protesters on the steps of the U.S. Capitol Building

Members of the Michigan Militia

SECTION 1: Extended-Response Questions

SECTION 2: The Core Democratic Values

SECTION 3: A Sample Extended-Response Question

EXTENDED-RESPONSE QUESTIONS

The last type of question on the Social Studies MEAP Test is known as an **extended-response question**. These questions will ask you to write a short essay or letter about a **public policy issue**. There will be two of these on the test. You will be given about 20 minutes to answer each question. This chapter will show you how to answer an extended-response question, in three steps:

- ✦ First, you will learn what a "public policy issue" is;
- ✦ Second, you will identify *core democratic values*; and
- ✦ Third, you will analyze a public policy issue and examine a sample extended-response question.

DEFINING A "PUBLIC POLICY" ISSUE

An **issue** is a topic about which people have different points of view. A **public policy issue** is an issue of concern to an entire community. The community could be your town, your state, or the whole nation. Public policy issues usually center around whether the government should pass a law or take some other action to resolve a problem. Public policy issues are often stated as a "should" question:

- ✦ *Should* the community ban the use of skateboards on public property?
- ✦ *Should* students be required to wear uniforms in school?
- ✦ *Should* the national government limit the violence shown on television?

There is NO "right" or "wrong" side to an issue. People will take different positions based on their points of view. When asked to state your position on an issue, you should present the opinion you think is best. Then you *must* support your position with reasons and facts.

THE CORE DEMOCRATIC VALUES

In making decisions about public issues, Americans apply a set of common values. A **value** is something we consider important and worthwhile. We refer to the values of American society as the **core democratic values**.

The idea that every person has worth and dignity is one of the most basic of our core democratic values. American society is based on the principle that the importance of every person should be recognized and respected by others.

Our core democratic values are found mainly in two key documents from our past: the **Declaration of Independence** and the **U.S. Constitution**. These documents can be thought of as two mighty pillars supporting our society.

The U.S. Constitution being adopted at Independence Hall in Philadelphia, September 17, 1787

In the Declaration of Independence, Americans declared their freedom from Great Britain. The Declaration also announced that there were certain basic truths about people that all governments should recognize. One of these truths was that the purpose of a government should be to protect the "life, liberty and pursuit of happiness" of its citizens.

As you know, the U.S. Constitution later established the basic system of American government. It also guaranteed certain rights to all Americans. A **right** is the freedom to do (or *not* to do) something. Our most important constitutional rights are found in five areas:

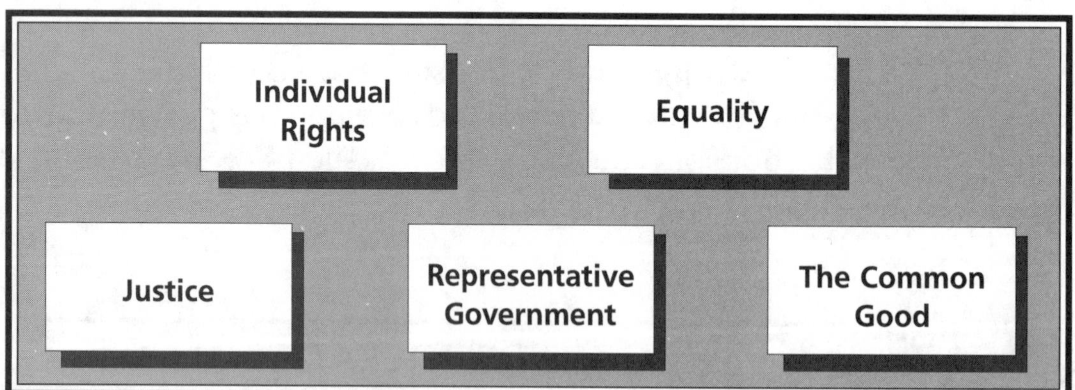

On the following page is a chart listing core democratic values that will appear on the Social Studies MEAP Test. In each extended-response question, you will be asked to refer to at least one of these core democratic values and to explain how it supports your position.

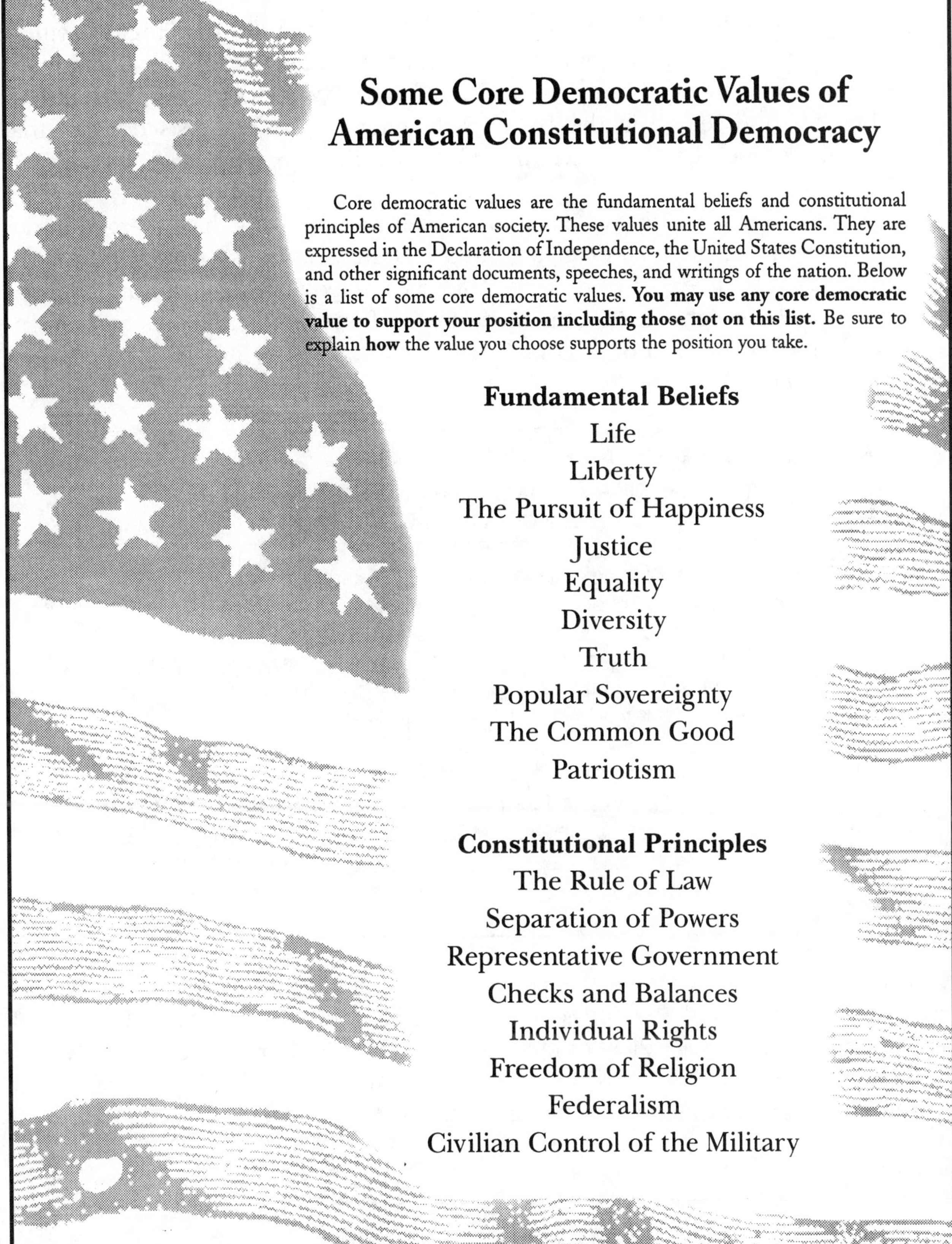

Some Core Democratic Values of American Constitutional Democracy

Core democratic values are the fundamental beliefs and constitutional principles of American society. These values unite all Americans. They are expressed in the Declaration of Independence, the United States Constitution, and other significant documents, speeches, and writings of the nation. Below is a list of some core democratic values. **You may use any core democratic value to support your position including those not on this list.** Be sure to explain **how** the value you choose supports the position you take.

Fundamental Beliefs

Life
Liberty
The Pursuit of Happiness
Justice
Equality
Diversity
Truth
Popular Sovereignty
The Common Good
Patriotism

Constitutional Principles

The Rule of Law
Separation of Powers
Representative Government
Checks and Balances
Individual Rights
Freedom of Religion
Federalism
Civilian Control of the Military

INDIVIDUAL RIGHTS

Our tradition of individual rights began in the 1600s when the first English settlers came to North America. Many of the first colonists left England in search of a place where they could practice their own religion freely. People of many different religious beliefs soon settled in the colonies. Eventually, the colonists decided that everyone should be free to practice his or her own religion.

Based on individual rights in England, as well as new rights that emerged under colonial conditions, the American colonists recognized that citizens should have other rights besides freedom of religion. After the United States became an independent country, these rights were guaranteed by the first ten amendments to the Constitution, known as the **Bill of Rights**. The rights listed below are guaranteed by the First Amendment.

Freedom of the Press. People have the right to print their ideas and beliefs even if they criticize the government.

Freedom of Speech. People have the right to express their ideas and beliefs in public.

Freedom of Assembly. People have the right to hold public meetings, even if their purpose is to protest government actions.

Freedom to Petition Government. People have the right to write to government leaders and ask them to make changes.

EQUALITY

American society is based on the cooperation of many different groups. We all expect to be treated fairly by our government and by our fellow citizens. Because of equality, everyone — regardless of race, ethnic background, or gender — has "equal protection" under the law. This means that the government cannot pass laws that unfairly favor some groups while harming others.

JUSTICE

Americans believe that justice must be administered fairly, as expressed in the phrase "due process of law." This means the government must follow specific procedures when it accuses someone of a crime or wants to take away someone's property for the public good. For example, people accused of a crime must be tried by a jury of fellow citizens, according to established rules. They also have the right *not* to testify at their own trial. The following graphic organizer will help you to remember some of the most important rights of individuals accused of a crime:

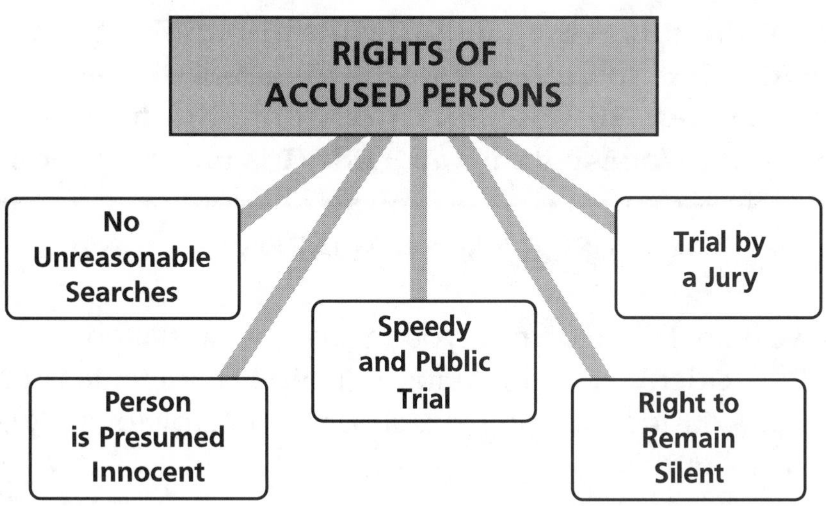

It is useful to remember that the protection of the rights of accused people sends a powerful message throughout society. Individual rights are important and must be respected. Our laws attempt to make sure that the government cannot punish people for crimes they did not commit. Each of us feels safer because we know that we cannot be arrested or punished without due process of law.

REPRESENTATIVE GOVERNMENT

A belief in **popular sovereignty** *(rule by the people)* and **representative government** forms another part of our core democratic values. Americans believe that government should serve the interests of the people. Voters elect representatives to run the government and to carry out the will of the citizens.

THE COMMON GOOD

Although Americans prize individual freedom, they also value the community. It is only by acting together that Americans can develop resources, increase knowledge, run a modern economy, and defend their country. For this reason, promoting the **common good** — the well-being of the entire community — is another core democratic value. Sometimes a public issue arises when promoting the common good would mean restricting some individual rights.

SECTION 3

A SAMPLE EXTENDED-RESPONSE QUESTION

This sample question is similar to the extended-response questions on the MEAP Test.

Directions: Read the following imaginary information about a public policy issue. Use it with what you already know to complete the tasks that follow. You should take about 20 minutes to complete both Task I and Task II. Task I is a selected-response item and Task II is an extended-response item.

USE OF SKATEBOARDS

Earlier this year in Mapletown a young boy on a skateboard accidentally crashed into an elderly lady, breaking her hip. This incident prompted the town council to consider banning skateboards in Mapletown. Read the information below about this issue.

DATA SECTION.

PART A Before making a decision, the town council conducted an opinion poll. People of all ages were asked whether skateboarding should be banned in Mapletown. The graph below shows the results:

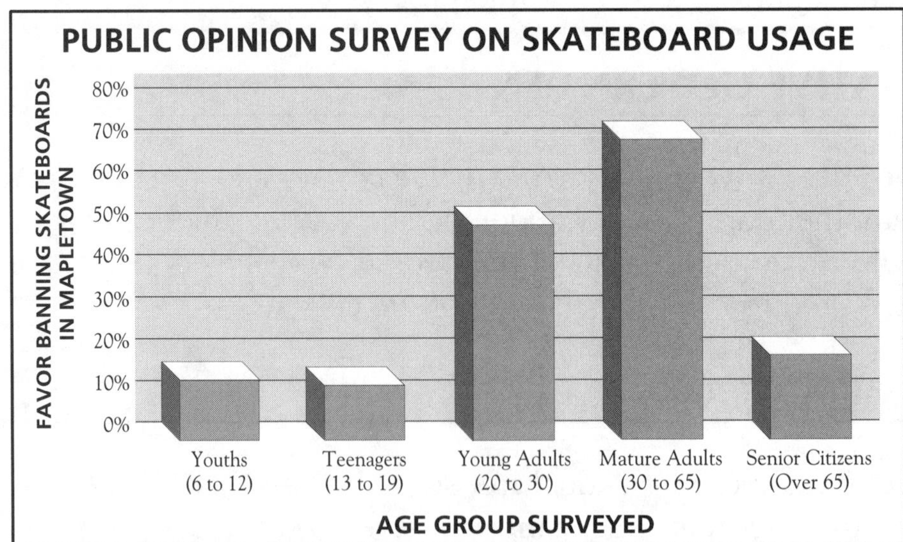

PART B In making its decision, the town council was provided with the following information about accidents from towns in the same county.

(continued...)

LINCOLN COUNTY ANNUAL ACCIDENT REPORT

Town	Bicycle Accidents	Skateboard Accidents	Auto Accidents
Mapletown	3	1	17
Hillcrest	2	0	10
Newburg	5	2	25

COMPLETE THE FOLLOWING TASKS:

Task I: Interpreting Information

Study the information in Part A of the Data Section. Which of the following statements best describes the *relationship* between the **use of skateboards** and the **age groups expressing opinions**?

A The two groups most opposed to banning the use of skateboards were youths and young adults.
B Mature adults and senior citizens were the two groups most in favor of banning the use of skateboards.
C Most mature adults were in favor of banning the use of skateboards.
D More than 70 percent of teenagers favored banning the use of skateboards.

Task II: Taking A Stand

You will now take a stand on the following public issue: **Should Mapletown ban the use of skateboards?** You may either support or oppose skateboard use in Mapletown. Write a letter expressing your view on the issue to your town council. Use information to provide reasons that support your position.

You will be graded on the following, so be sure your letter includes each of the elements listed below:

- A clear statement of your position.
- Supporting information using core democratic values of American constitutional democracy. (See page 109 for examples.)
- Supporting knowledge from history, geography, civics, or economics that you already know. (It is not enough to state only your opinion.)
- Supporting information from the Data Section (Part A and Part B).

Remember to: Use complete sentences.
Explain your reasons in detail.
Write or print neatly on the lines provided.

(continued...)

Should Mapletown ban the use of skateboards?

Dear Town Council Members:

Use this checklist to review your letter.

- ❑ I stated my position clearly.
- ❑ I supported my position with reference to at least one core democratic value of American constitutional democracy.
- ❑ I supported my position with knowledge from history, geography, civics, or economics that I already knew.
- ❑ I supported my position with information from the Data Section.

As you can see from this sample, extended-response questions consist of two main parts: Task I and Task II. Let's take a closer look at each of these.

ANSWERING THE QUESTION: TASK I

Task I tests your understanding of information in the Data Section. As explained in the previous chapter on inquiry, Task I asks you to make a **connection** or to find a **relationship** between two variables (age groups and opinions about banning skateboards). This part of the task tests your ability to see common patterns in specific examples. Let's focus on the two pieces of evidence in the Data Section.

Part A contains a bar graph showing how various age groups feel about the proposed ban on skateboarding. Task I in this question asks you to interpret the data in Part A. Look at the specific age groups in the bar graph in Part A. You should notice that young people generally oppose the ban, while mature adults generally favor it. However, senior citizens generally oppose the ban. The correct answer for Task I is choice **C**. All the other statements are incorrect, according to the bar graph.

Part B contains a table showing the number of accidents in Mapletown and two other towns in the same county. If you look at the specific number of each type of accident (bicycle, skateboard, and automobile accidents), you will notice that skateboards caused the least number of accidents.

ANSWERING THE QUESTION: TASK II

Task II asks you to take a stand on a public policy issue by expressing your opinion in writing. In your written answer, you must:

- ✦ base your opinion on one of the core democratic values;
- ✦ support your position with information from the Data Section; and
- ✦ support your answer with information from your knowledge of social studies.

USING THE 5-S APPROACH

Before you begin Task II of an extended-response question, you should take a few minutes to jot down some notes to help you write your answer. One simple way to remember what to do is think of the **5 S's**:

State your position.

Select a Core Democratic Value to support your opinion.

Support your position with evidence from the Data Section.

Support your position with evidence from your social studies knowledge.

Summarize your argument.

Let's see how using this method can bring all of these factors together into a logical, well-organized letter.

PRE-WRITING NOTES

State your Position

After reading the question and analyzing the Data Section, you should form your own opinion. In our sample question, that means you would either support or oppose the ban on skateboards.

Select a Core Democratic Value

Your position must be supported by a core democratic value. Although a long list of core democratic values exists (see. p. 109), most issues will focus on five main values.

1. **INDIVIDUAL RIGHTS/LIBERTY.** Many of these rights, such as free speech and freedom of religion, are guaranteed in the Bill of Rights. If the question deals with limiting the freedom of individuals, you can refer to this core democratic value. Here, you might say that the proposed ban on skateboarding would unfairly limit a person's freedom to use a skateboard.

2. **EQUALITY.** The 14th Amendment to the Constitution states that all Americans must be treated fairly and equally under the law. If the question deals with treating some groups differently than others, you might refer to this core democratic value. Here, you might say that it is unfair to restrict skateboarders but not automobile drivers, since automobiles cause many more accidents than skateboards do.

(continued...)

3. **JUSTICE.** Americans are very concerned with protecting their liberties and property from unfair acts by government. If the question deals with taking away the property or rights of a person or group, then the core democratic value of justice may be involved. Here, you might say that it is unjust to ban skateboarding without having a public hearing in which people who use skateboards can express their views.

4. **REPRESENTATIVE GOVERNMENT**. The United States has a representative government. This means the government usually does what the majority of people, who elect government officials, want to do. If you decided to support the ban on skateboarding, you could refer to this core democratic value, because one of the pieces of data in the Data Section shows that the majority of the adult community wants the ban on skateboarding.

5. **THE COMMON GOOD**. Our democratic society tries to do what is best for the community. Therefore, if the question deals with something that you think would benefit the community, support your position with this core democratic value. Here, you could say that the proposed ban on skateboards would reduce accidents and make Mapletown a safer place. Or, if you oppose the ban, you could say that the common good sometimes comes into conflict with another core democratic value — individual rights — and you believe individual rights are more important in this case.

Support Your Position with Evidence from the Data Section

Return to the Data Section. Look for information to use that supports your point of view. For example, in this case the majority of adults wanted a ban on skateboarding. On the other hand, the data also shows that bicycles cause many more accidents than skateboards, yet the town is not considering a ban on bicycles.

Support Your Position with Your Social Studies Knowledge

To support your position using your social studies knowledge, you should keep in mind some of the basic concepts of geography, history, economics, and civics. For example:

Geography. Look at the situation in the question. Are any of the five themes of geography involved? If so, identify which ones. For example, we know that people are influenced by their environment. You might mention how the people of an area would be affected by a proposed policy change.

(continued...)

History. Again, look at the question. Have you ever studied a past situation similar to the public issue described in the question? It is especially relevant to draw on your history knowledge when two sides are opposed to each other. You might refer to groups that once opposed each other and then resolved their conflict through a compromise — as Michigan and Ohio did over the Toledo Strip.

Economics. Again, think carefully about the issue presented in the question. If it involves spending government money, think about how the government will have to raise the money — probably through taxes. You might also refer to the idea of "opportunity cost," since every decision to buy something involves opportunity costs. If the government spends money to solve the problem in the question, what other problems might go unsolved for lack of money?

Civics. As always, start by looking at the public policy issue in the question and the evidence in the Data Section. Will the local, state, or national government be involved? If so, mention what powers or roles the government will play in addressing the issue. Would government be going beyond its constitutional powers by adopting the change suggested in the question? In our sample question, it is helpful to recall that one of the main roles of local government is to ensure public safety.

Summarize your Argument

At the end of your response, you should once again state your position on the issue. This should be done in an affirmative way (not saying what you are *against,* but what you are *in favor of*). For example:

> "As a result of the arguments I have presented in this letter, I feel that the town council should ban the use of skateboards."

WRITING YOUR LETTER OR ESSAY

The last step is to convert your pre-writing notes into a letter (or essay, depending on which type of writing the question asks for). As you write, remember to follow the same **5-S** approach you just read about.

Dear Town Council Members:

I believe that skateboarding should be banned in Mapletown. I feel this way for a number of reasons.

State your position

One of our most important core democratic values is representative government. This means that the majority should rule. The council represents Mapletown's voters, who are adults. Since most voters in Mapletown want to ban skateboards, this is what the council should do.

Select a core democratic value to support your position

My opinion is further supported by the survey results in the Data Section. They show that a majority of adults in Mapletown want a ban on skateboarding. I think adults know more about safety than children do. I am sure most adults feel that skateboarding is dangerous. One person has already been injured.

Select supporting evidence from the Data Section

We know from civics that one job of our local town government is to protect public safety. By banning skateboards, the council will meet its responsibility on public safety.

Select supporting evidence from your social studies knowledge

In conclusion, I would like to remind you that we live in a democratic society, and the council should do what most voters want. As a result of the arguments I have presented in this letter, I feel that the council should ban the use of skateboards.

Summarize your positon

Sincerely yours,

____

(Sign your name)

REMEMBER: Use this basic framework in writing your answer to **any** extended-response question.

CHAPTER 11

A PRACTICE MEAP TEST IN SOCIAL STUDIES

You have now reviewed what you need to know to do well on the 5th grade MEAP Test in Social Studies. At this point, you are ready to take a practice test.

You should take the following test under "test conditions." This means taking the entire test in a quiet room. Complete the test in two separate sessions, as indicated. This will give you a feeling for what the actual test will be like. Taking this practice test will reduce any anxiety you might have about the real test.

The practice test will also help you to identify areas that you still need to study and review. For example, after taking the test you may find you had problems answering selected-response questions on history or extended-response questions on public policy issues. In that case, you should review again the sections of this book focusing on those types of questions.

Good luck on this practice test!

DAY ONE: SOCIAL STUDIES ASSESSMENT

Instructions to the Student

There are three types of questions on this test: **selected-response, constructed-response**, and **extended-response**.

- **Selected-response** questions will ask you first to read a passage, map, chart, or table. After studying this prompt, read the questions and choose the best answer from among four answer choices.
- **Constructed-response** questions will ask you to explain a conclusion, provide examples, complete a chart, interpret information, or give a reason for an answer you have given.
- **Extended-response** questions require you to write an answer that is more detailed and requires more thinking. These items ask you to interpret information from a set of data on an imaginary policy issue, identify a relationship presented in the Data Section, take a position for or against the policy, and give reasons supporting your position.

Use a separate answer sheet (see page 154) to mark your choices for the **selected-response** questions. Fill in the circle for your choice on the answer sheet. Remember to fill in the circle completely and cleanly, erasing any stray lines or marks.

Space is provided in the test section for you to write your answers to **constructed-response** and **extended-response** items.

Read all directions for these items carefully.

If you finish early, you may check your work for Day One **only**. Do **not** go ahead and work on the Day Two section of this test.

Geography

Directions: Study the following photographs and use them with what you already know to answer the questions that follow.

#1

#5

#2

#6

#3

#7

#4

#8

Geography

1 Photo #1 was MOST likely taken in the

A Lower Peninsula
B Florida Everglades
C Appalachian Mountains
D Upper Peninsula

II.4.LE.4

2 Which picture illustrates a major Michigan industry of the mid-1800s?

A Photo #2 **C** Photo #4
B Photo #3 **D** Photo #5

II.4.LE.3

3 The industry shown in Photo #3 MOST helped the economic development of which city in Michigan?

A Detroit
B Sault Ste. Marie
C Grand Rapids
D Battle Creek

II.3.LE.1

4 If you wanted to visit your state senator at work in the legislature, which picture shows where you would go?

A Photo #1 **C** Photo #7
B Photo #6 **D** Photo #8

II.1.LE.2

5 Which picture might be used to represent the unity of the Upper and Lower Peninsulas?

A Photo #1 **C** Photo #6
B Photo #2 **D** Photo #8

II.3.LE.3

Geography

Directions: Study the following map and use it with what you already know to answer the questions that follow.

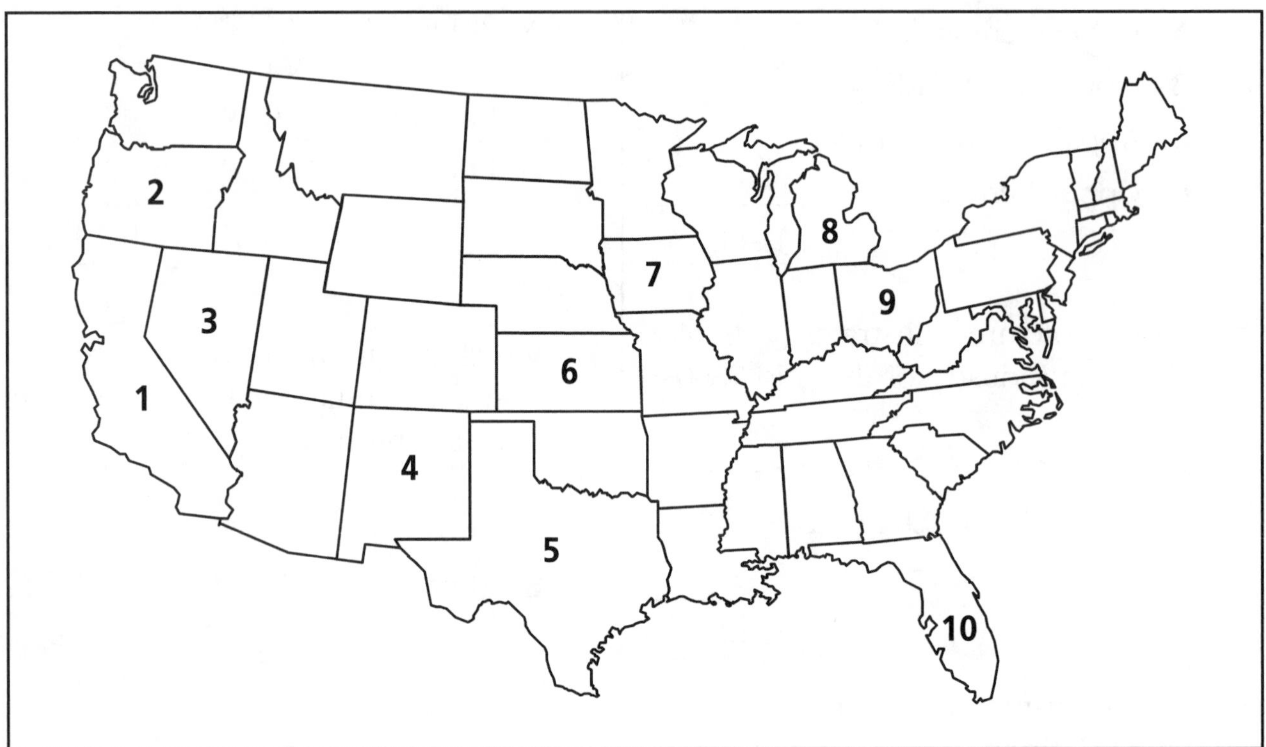

6 Which pair of states are MOST influenced by trade with Canada?

A State 2 and State 9
B State 8 and State 9
C State 1 and State 6
D State 3 and State 4

II.3.LE.1

7 Which state is a major center of lumber production?

A State 2
B State 3
C State 4
D State 6

II.2.LE.2

8 Which state borders four of the five Great Lakes?

A State 2
B State 8
C State 9
D State 10

II.4.LE.3

9 Which state's climate is MOST influenced by the Gulf of Mexico and the Atlantic Ocean?

A State 1
B State 4
C State 5
D State 10

II.4.LE.6

10 Which of the following BEST describes the geography of State 6 and State 7?

A They are both near large bodies of water.
B They are both located near large mountain ranges.
C They both have favorable soil conditions for grain production.
D They both have large deposits of gold.

II.3.LE.1

Geography

Directions: You should take about 5 minutes to analyze the following map and use it with what you already know to complete this task.

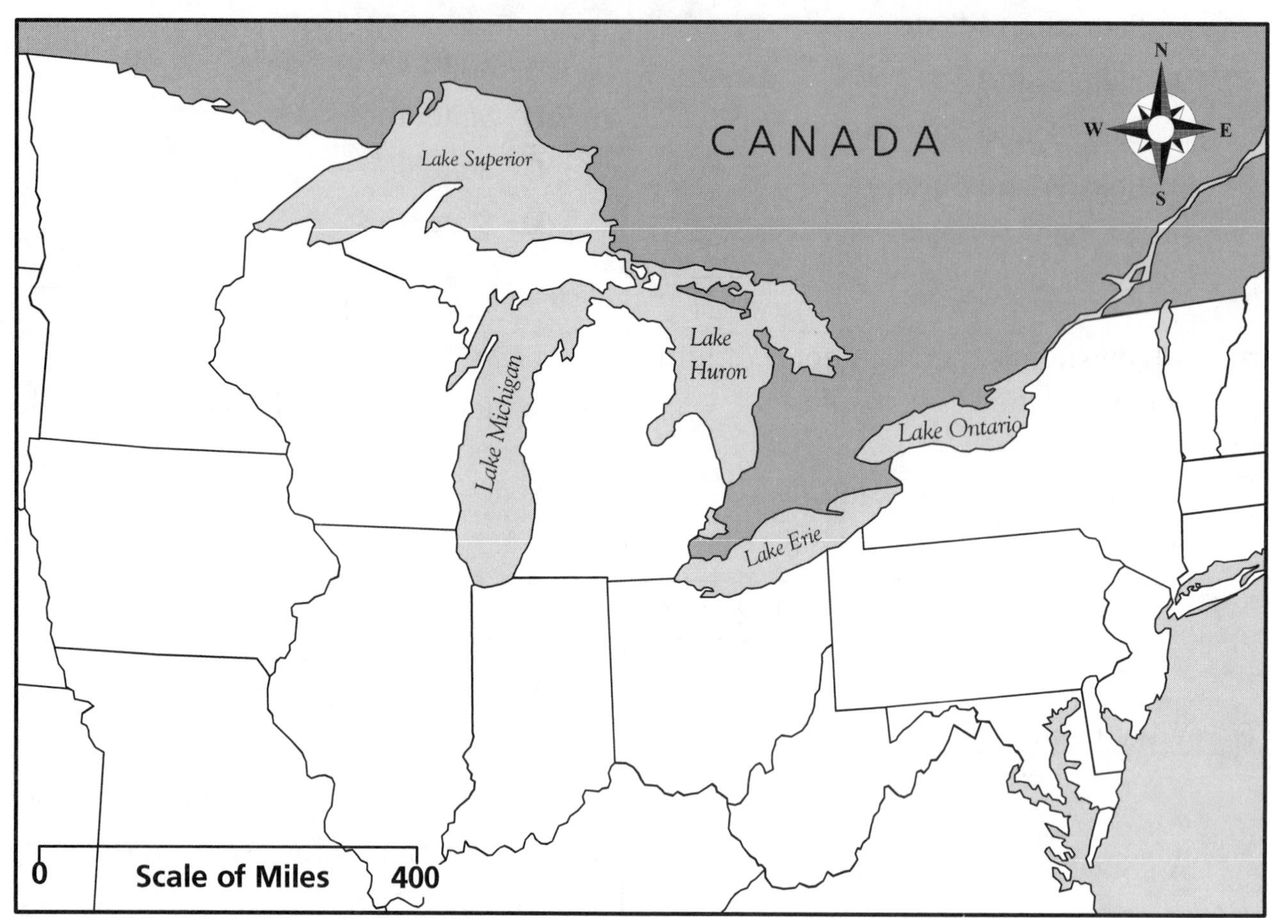

Geography

11 The Great Lakes ecosystem consists of states in the United States and two Canadian provinces. On the lines provided, identify two states in the Great Lakes ecosystem. Then explain how the Great Lakes ecosystem has affected lifestyles (occupations, recreation, clothing, etc.) in the region.

Identification of two states in the Great Lakes ecosystem:

State #1: ____________________ State #2: ________________________

II.2.LE.3

Explanation of how the Great Lakes ecosystem has affected lifestyles in the region.

____

____

____

____

____

____

____

____

II.2.LE.1/
II.2.LE.2

History

Directions: Study the following timeline and use it with what you already know to answer the questions that follow.

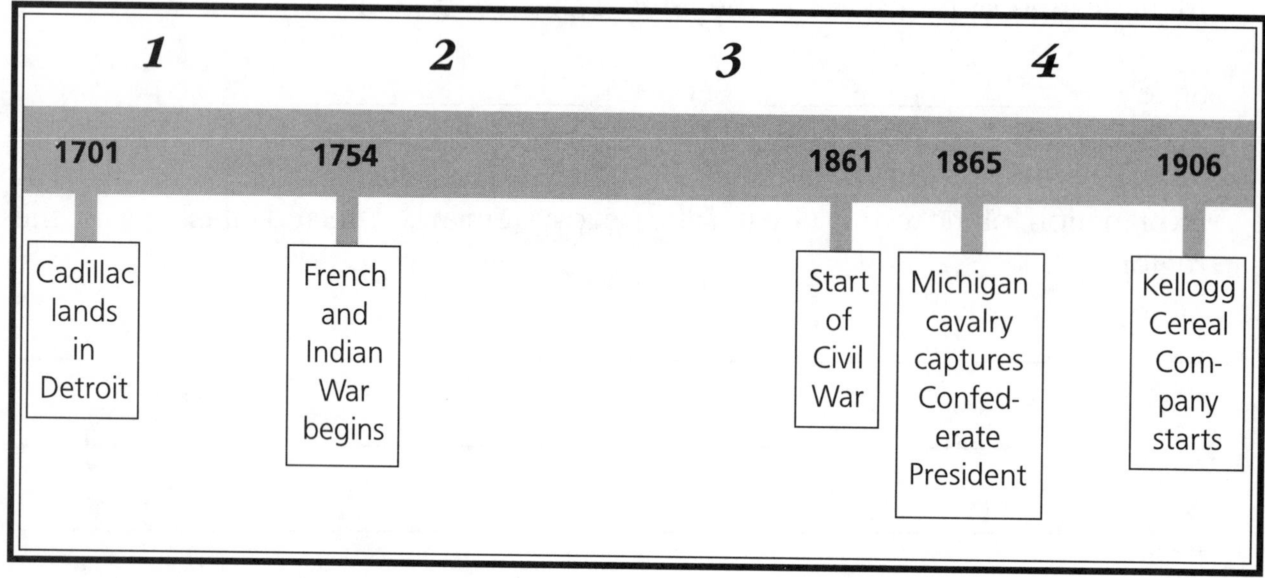

12 According to the timeline, which event occurred in the 20th century?

A Cadillac landed in Detroit
B Start of Civil War
C French and Indian War began
D The Kellogg Cereal Company started

I.1.LE.1

13 Which number above the timeline represents where you would place the year Michigan became a state in 1837?

A Number 1 **C** Number 3
B Number 2 **D** Number 4

I.1.LE.2

14 Which would be the BEST title for the events on the timeline?

A Important Events of 19th-Century Michigan
B Major Events of the Midwest
C Selected Events in the History of Michigan
D Major Events in American History

I.2.LE.1

15 Which event occurred AFTER the time period shown on this timeline?

A Ralph Bunche was appointed U.S. Ambassador to the United Nations
B Pontiac's War began
C Copper was discovered in the Upper Peninsula
D Étienne Brûlé visited the Michigan area

I.1.LE.3

16 Which of the following statements does NOT belong on this timeline?

A Michigan is the best place to manufacture cars
B German immigrants settle in Frankenmuth
C Elizabeth Chandler starts the Michigan Anti-Slavery Society
D Congress settles dispute over the Toledo Strip

I.3.LE.2

History

Directions: Study the following map. Use it with what you already know to answer the questions that follow.

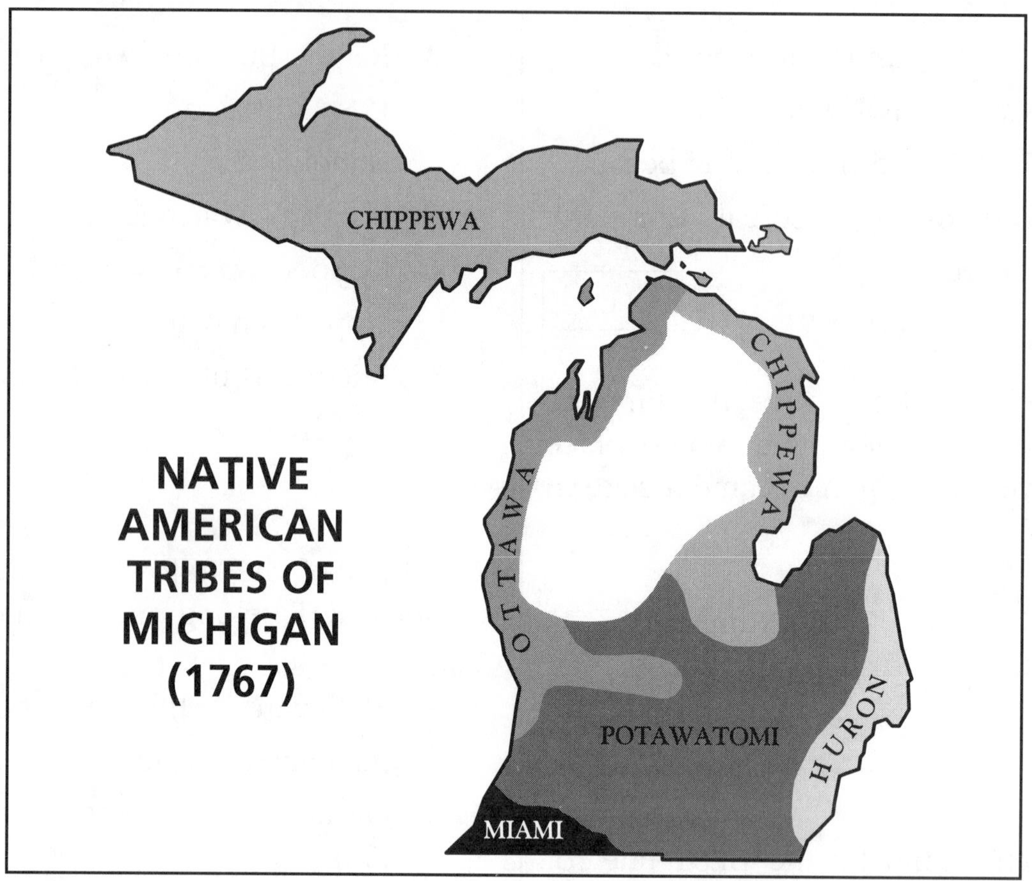

17 Approximately how much time passed between the date shown on the map and the start of the 20th century?

A one century

B seven decades

C thirteen decades

D three centuries

I.1.LE.1

18 Which of the following statements BEST describes the tribes shown on the map?

A They lived in dwellings covered with branches and strips of bark.

B They lived in houses known as pueblos.

C They hunted alligators and planted rice as a way of life.

D They carved totem poles.

I.1.LE.1

19 Which of the following is a PRIMARY source about the lifestyles of the people shown on the map?

A a newspaper article written today about Chippewa lifestyles in the 1800s

B an almanac giving the number of Huron tribe members who lived in Michigan in the late 1800s

C a photograph of modern school children dressed in traditional Chippewa clothing

D a letter from an early pioneer describing Native Americans he met on the Upper Peninsula

I.3.LE.1

20 Which FACT can you tell about early Native Americans of Michigan from looking at this map?

A The Hurons lived in an area near present-day Detroit.

B The Miami lived in both the Upper and Lower Peninsulas.

C The Menominee occupied the largest area in Michigan.

D Native American tribes shared a common lifestyle.

I.2.LE.3

21 In which of the following types of homes would MOST of the groups shown on this map have lived?

A plantation   **C** igloo

B pueblo   **D** wigwam

I.2.LE.3

History

Directions: You should take about 5 minutes to look over the following map and use it with what you already know to complete this task.

LOCATION OF SOME MAJOR ETHNIC GROUPS IN MICHIGAN

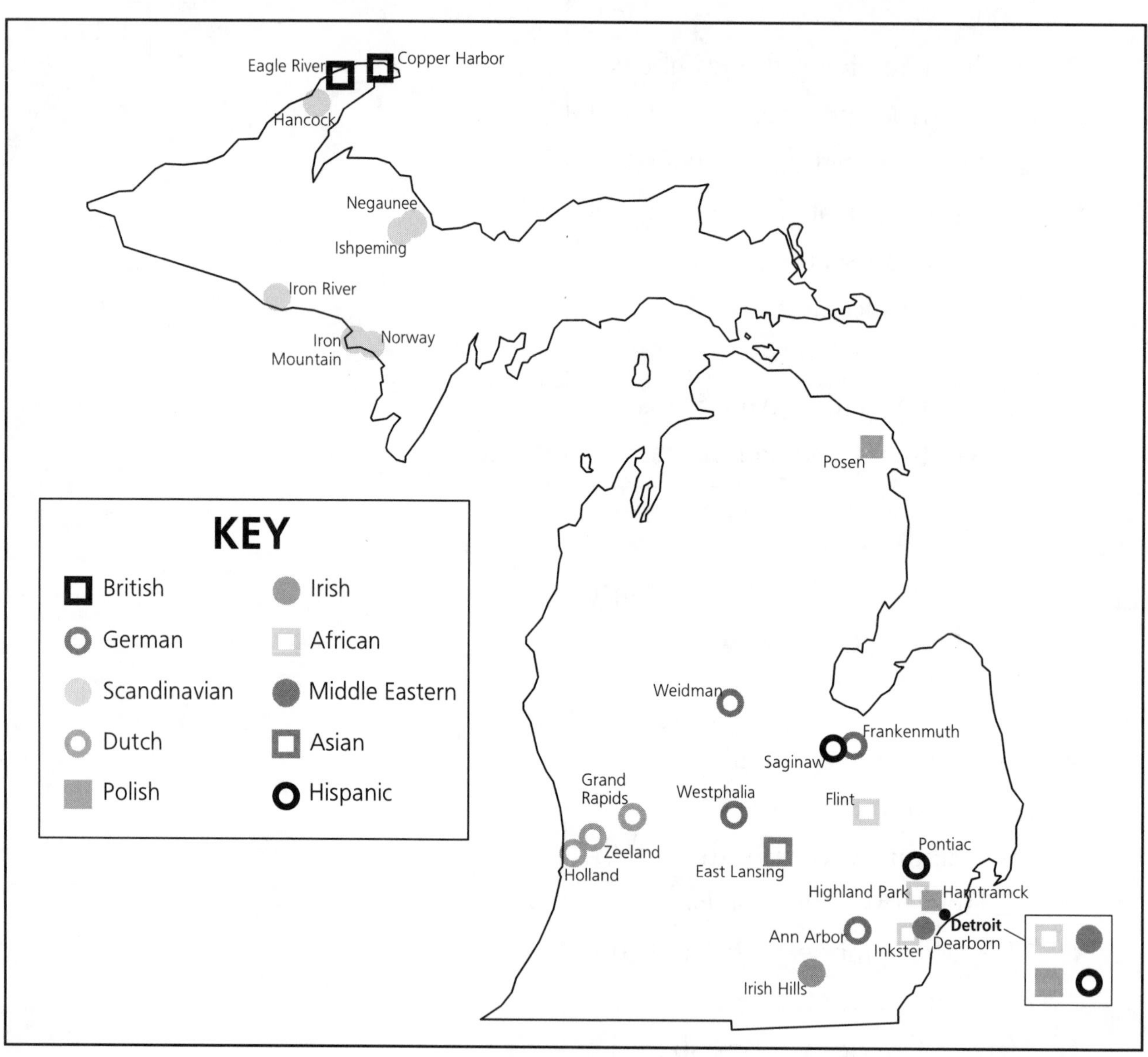

History

22 Many different ethnic groups have emigrated to the United States and Michigan. Once here, they have contributed to Michigan's rich heritage. The map shows the main population centers of some of Michigan's largest ethnic communities.

On the lines provided, identify one ethnic community from the Upper Peninsula and one from the Lower Peninsula. Then select either one of these ethnic groups and show how that group has made a contribution to Michigan's cultural heritage.

Identification of an ethnic group on the Upper Peninsula: ________________

Identification of an ethnic group on the Lower Peninsula: ________________

Explanation of how one of these groups has contributed to Michigan's cultural heritage:

____

____

____

____

____

____

____

I.2.LE.2

Inquiry and Decision Making

Directions: Read the following information about a public policy issue. Use it with what you already know to complete the tasks that follow. You should take about 20 minutes to complete both Task I and Task II. Task I is a selected-response item and Task II is an extended-response item.

BUILDING A SPORTS COMPLEX

There is only one playground in Elmwood. The school board has proposed building a sports complex next to the school. The issue has caused much discussion in the community. Read the following information about building the sports complex.

DATA SECTION

PART A The school board took a survey of people in the community. The survey asked people the following question: "Do you favor building a sports complex for the school district?" Here are the results of the survey:

PERCENTAGE OF THOSE WHO FAVOR BUILDING A SPORTS COMPLEX

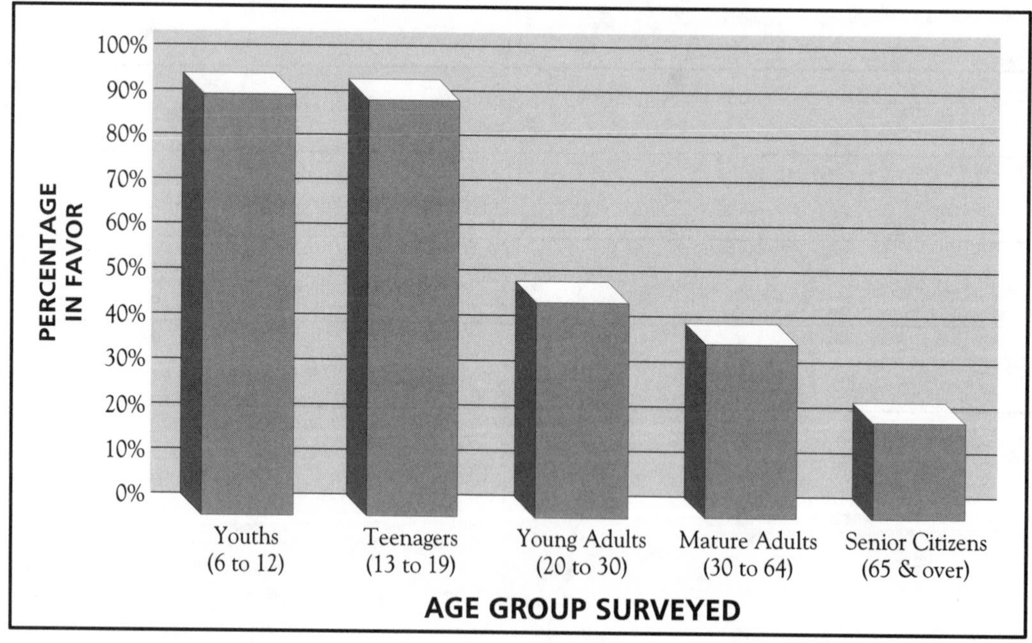

PART B In considering this proposal, the town council was provided with the following information about financing the construction of the new sports complex:

IMPACT ON THE TOWN'S PROPERTY TAX

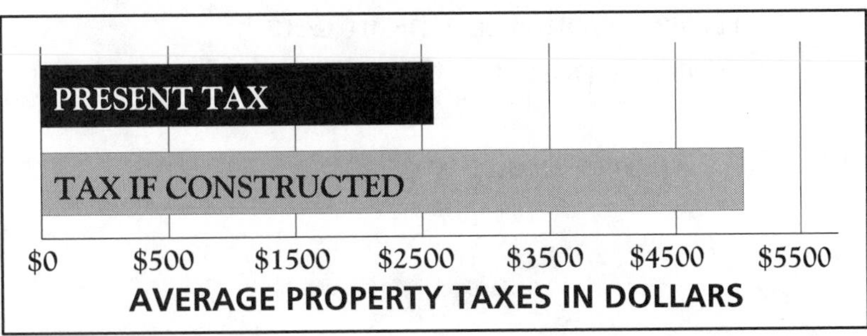

COMPLETE THE FOLLOWING TASKS:

Task I: Interpreting Information

23 Study the information in Part A of the Data Section. Which statement best describes the *relationship* between **age** and **opinion about building the sports complex?** Be sure to mark your answer on the answer sheet.

A More than 30% of teenagers opposed building the sports complex.
B Most mature adults and senior citizens favored building the sports complex.
C The two groups most in favor of building the sports complex were youths and mature adults.
D Most adults were against building the sports complex.

Task II: Taking a Stand

24 You will now take a stand on the following public issue: **Should Elmwood build a sports complex?** You may either support or oppose building the sports complex. Write a letter to your local newspaper expressing your opinion. Include information that supports your position.

You will be graded on the following, so be sure your letter includes each of the elements listed below:

- A clear statement of your position.
- Supporting information using core democratic values of American constitutional democracy. (See page 109 for examples.)
- Supporting knowledge from history, geography, civics, or economics that you already know. (It is not enough to state only your opinion.)
- Supporting information from the Data Section.

Inquiry and Decision Making

Remember to: Use complete sentences.
Explain your reasons in detail.
Write or print neatly on the lines provided below.

Should Elmwood build a sports complex?

Dear Newspaper Editor:

Use this checklist to review your letter.

- ❑ I stated my position clearly.
- ❑ I supported my position with reference to at least one core democratic value of American constitutional democracy.
- ❑ I supported my position with knowledge from history, geography, civics, or economics that I already knew.
- ❑ I supported my position with information from the Data Section.

STOP

Day Two: Social Studies Assessment

Instructions to the Student

There are three types of questions on this test: **selected-response, constructed-response**, and **extended-response**.

- **Selected-response** questions will ask you first to read a passage, map, chart, or table. After studying this prompt, read the questions and choose the best answer from among four answer choices.

- **Constructed-response** questions will ask you to explain a conclusion, provide examples, complete a chart, interpret information, or give a reason for an answer you have given.

- **Extended-response** questions require you to write an answer that is more detailed and requires more thinking. These items ask you to interpret information from a set of data on an imaginary policy issue, identify a relationship presented in the Data Section, take a position for or against the policy, and give reasons supporting your position.

Use a separate answer sheet to mark your choice for the **selected-response** questions. Fill in the circle for your choice on the answer sheet. Remember to fill in the circle completely and cleanly, erasing any stray lines or marks.

Space is provided in the test section for you to write your answers to **constructed-response** and **extended-response** items.

Read all directions for these items carefully.

If you finish early, you may check your work for Day Two **only**. Do **not** work on the Day One section of this test.

Economics

Directions: Study the following table and use it with what you already know to answer the questions that follow.

Following is a list of projects that your town government is considering. However, the citizens of your town have approved raising no more than $5,000,000 for new projects.

TOWN PROJECTS UNDER CONSIDERATION

PROPOSED PROJECT	COST OF THE PROJECT
Project A: Expand the town dump	$2,900,000
Project B: Increase aid to the senior citizens center	$5,000,000
Project C: Add more firefighters and police officers	$3,400,000
Project D: Build a new stadium for the Little League	$4,100,000
Project E: Repave the town streets	$4,600,000

Economics

25 Which principle of economics is BEST illustrated by the choices facing the town?

A supply and demand
B factors of production
C scarcity
D interdependence

IV.1.LE.1

26 Suppose the town government decided to spend the money on Project B instead of Project A. The fact that the town did not choose to spend the money on Project A would illustrate the concept of

A supply and demand
B opportunity cost
C factors of production
D interdependence

IV.1.LE.2

27 From which power does the town government get its authority to raise money for the proposed projects?

A the power to tax
B the power to maintain peace
C the power to ensure the welfare of its citizens
D the power to regulate local trade

IV.3.LE.2

28 The proposed projects in the town's budget are examples of

A international trade
B a market economy
C public goods and services
D consumer credit

IV.3.LE.1

29 Suppose the town wanted to make sure that the owners of any business working on Project D would be personally responsible for any accidents that might happen there. Which type of business should the town hire?

A a partnership
B a labor union
C a corporation
D a credit union

IV.2.LE.2

Economics

Directions: Study the following material. Use it with what you already know to answer the questions that follow.

Sarah's class wants to go on a field trip. To pay for the trip, Sarah and her classmates decide to raise the money they need by working.

ACTIVITY	PRICE
Activity 1. Lawn Services	$10 a lawn
Activity 2. Washing Cars	$4 a car
Activity 3. Walking Neighbors' Dogs	$6 an hour
Activity 4. Selling Handmade Greeting Cards	$4 per box of cards

Sarah and her classmates agree to take all their earnings and put them together for the trip. If anyone makes a mistake or delivers poor services, the entire class will share the responsibility and pay back the customer.

Economics

30 When working on Activity 4, Sarah and her classmates are acting as

A consumers **C** importers
B producers **D** exporters

IV.4.LE.2

31 What type of business organization is MOST similar to the agreement made by Sarah and her classmates?

A individual ownership
B partnership
C corporation
D labor union

IV.4.LE.1

32 Which is a factor of production involved in ALL FOUR of the activities Sarah and her classmates have decided to do?

A opportunity costs
B human capital
C global interdependence
D consumer credit

IV.4.LE.1

33 Which of the following would MOST likely result if other classes in the school offered to sell the same services?

A Prices for those services would probably go up.
B Prices for those services would probably go down.
C Demand for the services of Sarah's class would increase.
D Taxes on Sarah's class would increase.

IV.4.LE.1

34 Which of the following is the BEST example of opportunity cost?

A A parent spends money on Activity 1 instead of choosing Activity 2.
B Other classes become involved in Activity 2.
C Sarah's class joins with another class to sell other services in Activity 1.
D Prices are lowered on all goods and services involved with Activity 3.

IV.4.LE.2

Economics

Directions: You should take about 5 minutes to look at the following picture and use it with what you already know to complete this task.

Classic Oldsmobile from the 1930s
at the Ransom Olds Auto Museum in Lansing

Economics

35 On the lines provided, name **two** factors of production required to make the product in the photograph. For **each** factor of production named, describe how it contributed to the making of this product.

Identification of one factor of production, and description of how it contributed to making the product:

____

____

____

____

IV.2.LE.1

Identification of a second factor of production, and description of how it contributed to making the product:

____

____

____

____

IV.2.LE.1

Civics

Directions: Study the following material and use it with what you already know to answer the questions that follow.

THE ORGANIZATION OF AMERICAN GOVERNMENT

BRANCHES	Level 1: FEDERAL	LEVEL 2: STATE	LEVEL 3: LOCAL
	A. Congress	A. Michigan State Legislature	A. City Council
	B. The President	B. Governor of Michigan	B. Mayor
	C. U.S. Supreme Court	C. Michigan Supreme Court	C. City Courts

36 According to the chart, which of the following levels and branches of government would MOST likely be responsible for passing laws about Social Security?

A 1-A

B 1-B

C 2-B

D 2-C

III.4.LE.1

37 Which level and branch of government determines what subjects are required for high school students to graduate in Michigan?

A 1-A

B 2-A

C 2-C

D 3-C

III.1.LE.1

Civics

38 Which person or group is Commander-in-Chief of our country's armed forces?

A 1-A

B 2-B

C 2-C

D 3-B

III.1.LE.1

39 Which level and branch of government is responsible for deciding whether a law violates Michigan's state constitution?

A 2-A

B 2-B

C 2-C

D 3-C

III.3.LE.1

40 Which person or group in government is responsible for spending money to make sure that the streets in your community are cleaned?

A 1-A

B 2-B

C 2-C

D 3-B

III.4.LE.1

Civics

Directions: Study the following poster. Use it with what you already know to answer the questions that follow.

The following is a poster created to welcome people who have just become citizens of the United States.

CONGRATULATIONS ON BECOMING
AN AMERICAN CITIZEN!

You Have Now Earned the Right to:

1. *Freedom of Expression*
2. *Due Process Protection against Unlawful Arrest*
3. *Equal Protection of the Law*
4. *Privacy and Private Property*

41 The rights listed in the poster define

A the rights of government

B the rights of American citizens

C the branches of American government

D the responsibilities of citizenship

III.2.LE.2

42 In which document can you find the first and second rights listed on the poster?

A Declaration of Independence

B Articles of Confederation

C Bill of Rights

D Gettysburg Address

III.2.LE.2

43 Which reason BEST explains why all of these rights were created?

A to help attract immigrants to the United States

B to be like the British, who had similar rights

C to ensure that the national government would respect our individual freedoms

D to limit the rights of foreign-born citizens

III.2.LE.2

44 Which core democratic value protects our right to carry signs and banners that state our opposition to government policies?

A Right #1

B Right #2

C Right #3

D Right #4

III.2.LE.2

45 Throughout our nation's history, the rights listed in the poster have provided

A reasons why people chose to come to the United States

B a basis for helping homeless people in society

C warnings to show that criminal behavior would not be tolerated

D an example of the weaknesses of our national government

III.2.LE.2

Civics

Directions: You should take about 5 minutes to read the following letter and use it with what you already know to complete this task.

Dear José,

Our people have recently overthrown a dictator who ruled our nation for many years. My country is about to write a new Constitution, with a Bill of Rights similar to yours. I am curious to know what you think are the two most important freedoms or rights protected by your Bill of Rights.

Your pen pal,

Julia

46 On the lines provided, identify **two** rights listed in the Bill of Rights. Then write a letter of reply explaining why these two rights are so important.

Identification of two rights in the Bill of Rights:

Right #1: ______________________________

Right #2: ______________________________

III.2.LE.2

Complete the reply letter below. Be sure to explain why you believe the two rights you chose are of such importance.

Dear Julia,

I am writing to answer your letter. I have given this much thought, and I believe that two of the most important rights in the Bill of Rights are ____________________

____

____

____

____

____

____

____

____

____

____

Your pen pal,

José

Inquiry

Directions: You should take about five minutes to study the following material and use it with what you already know to complete these tasks.

AVERAGE JANUARY TEMPERATURES IN SELECTED NORTHEASTERN STATES

State	Temperature
Massachusetts	29° F
New York	25° F
Pennsylvania	28° F

AVERAGE JANUARY TEMPERATURES IN SELECTED SOUTHEASTERN STATES

State	Temperature
Alabama	50° F
Georgia	45° F
South Carolina	48° F

Task I:

47 Based on the table, which of the following statements best describes the relationship between **average temperatures** and the **location of states**?

A Average summer temperatures tend to be higher in the Southeast than in the Northeast.
B States in the Southeast tend to have higher January temperatures than states in the Northeast.
C States in the Northeast are warmer in the winter than states in the Southeast.
D States in the Southeast are just as warm in winter as they are in summer.

Task II:

48 Rank the states according to their average January temperatures, from highest to lowest. Write the name of each state in its correct location in the table below.

NORTHEASTERN AND SOUTHEASTERN STATES RANKED BY AVERAGE JANUARY TEMPERATURES

NORTHEASTERN STATES	SOUTHEASTERN STATES
1.	1.
2.	2.
3.	3.

Inquiry and Decision Making

Directions: Read the following imaginary information about a public policy issue. Use it with what you already know to complete the tasks that follow. You should take about 20 minutes to complete both Task I and Task II. Task I is a selected-response item and Task II is an extended-response item.

POLITICAL BUTTONS

The election of the student body president of Rosewood School is going to be a close contest. Five candidates represent different groups in the school. School administrators, in an attempt to reduce possible tensions, are considering a ban on the wearing of political campaign buttons by students. Read the following information.

DATA SECTION

PART A In making their decision, the Rosewood School Board was provided with the following information about four neighboring school districts:

SCHOOL DISTRICTS	NUMBER OF STUDENT FIGHTS
2 districts that allow political buttons	14
2 districts that ban political buttons	10

PART B The school board conducted a survey of community members. They were asked, "Do you favor banning the use of political buttons in school?" Here are the results of the survey:

THOSE WHO FAVOR BANNING POLITICAL BUTTONS

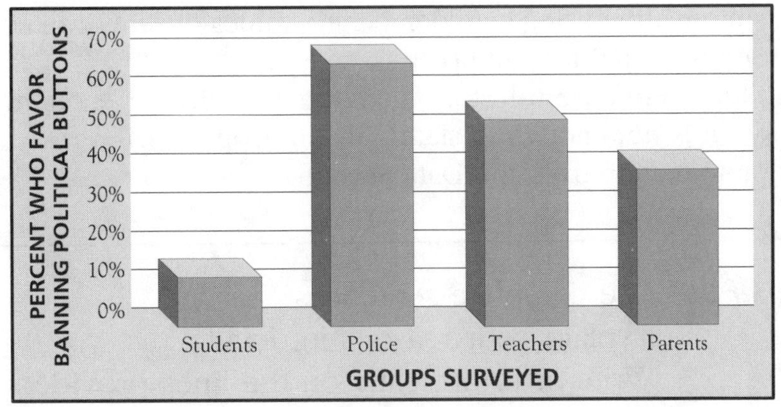

Inquiry and Decision Making

COMPLETE THE FOLLOWING TASKS:

Task I: Interpreting Information

49 Study the information in Part A of the Data Section. Which of the following statements best describes the *relationship* between **wearing political buttons** and **student fighting**? Be sure to mark your answer on the answer sheet.

A Fights among students were more frequent in districts where political buttons were allowed.

B Fights among students were less frequent in districts where political buttons were allowed.

C The same number of fights occurred in districts that allowed political buttons and districts that banned them.

D All school fights were caused by students wearing political buttons.

Task II: Taking a Stand

50 You will now take a stand on the following public issue: **Should Rosewood School District ban the wearing of political buttons by students?** You may either support or oppose this proposal. Write a letter expressing your opinion to the Rosewood School Board. Use information to provide reasons that support your position.

You will be graded on the following, so be sure your letter includes each of the elements listed below:

- A clear statement of your position.
- Supporting information using core democratic values of American constitutional democracy. (See page 109 for examples.)
- Supporting knowledge from history, geography, civics, or economics that you already know. (It is not enough to state only your opinion.)
- Supporting information from the Data Section.

Remember to: Use complete sentences.
Explain your reasons in detail.
Write or print neatly on the lines provided below

Inquiry and Decision Making

Should Rosewood School Board ban the wearing of political buttons?

Dear School Board Members:

Use this checklist to review your letter.

- ❑ I stated my position clearly.
- ❑ I supported my position with reference to at least one core democratic value of American constitutional democracy.
- ❑ I supported my position with knowledge from history, geography, civics, or economics that I already knew.
- ❑ I supported my position with information from the Data Section.

ANSWER SHEET FOR SELECTED-RESPONSE QUESTIONS IN PRACTICE SOCIAL STUDIES MEAP TEST, GRADE 5

Student________________________ Class________________________

Teacher________________________ Date________________________

DAY ONE

GEOGRAPHY					HISTORY				
1	Ⓐ	Ⓑ	Ⓒ	Ⓓ	12	Ⓐ	Ⓑ	Ⓒ	Ⓓ
2	Ⓐ	Ⓑ	Ⓒ	Ⓓ	13	Ⓐ	Ⓑ	Ⓒ	Ⓓ
3	Ⓐ	Ⓑ	Ⓒ	Ⓓ	14	Ⓐ	Ⓑ	Ⓒ	Ⓓ
4	Ⓐ	Ⓑ	Ⓒ	Ⓓ	15	Ⓐ	Ⓑ	Ⓒ	Ⓓ
5	Ⓐ	Ⓑ	Ⓒ	Ⓓ	16	Ⓐ	Ⓑ	Ⓒ	Ⓓ
6	Ⓐ	Ⓑ	Ⓒ	Ⓓ	17	Ⓐ	Ⓑ	Ⓒ	Ⓓ
7	Ⓐ	Ⓑ	Ⓒ	Ⓓ	18	Ⓐ	Ⓑ	Ⓒ	Ⓓ
8	Ⓐ	Ⓑ	Ⓒ	Ⓓ	19	Ⓐ	Ⓑ	Ⓒ	Ⓓ
9	Ⓐ	Ⓑ	Ⓒ	Ⓓ	20	Ⓐ	Ⓑ	Ⓒ	Ⓓ
10	Ⓐ	Ⓑ	Ⓒ	Ⓓ	21	Ⓐ	Ⓑ	Ⓒ	Ⓓ

INQUIRY AND DECISION MAKING				
23	Ⓐ	Ⓑ	Ⓒ	Ⓓ

DAY TWO

ECONOMICS					CIVICS				
25	Ⓐ	Ⓑ	Ⓒ	Ⓓ	36	Ⓐ	Ⓑ	Ⓒ	Ⓓ
26	Ⓐ	Ⓑ	Ⓒ	Ⓓ	37	Ⓐ	Ⓑ	Ⓒ	Ⓓ
27	Ⓐ	Ⓑ	Ⓒ	Ⓓ	38	Ⓐ	Ⓑ	Ⓒ	Ⓓ
28	Ⓐ	Ⓑ	Ⓒ	Ⓓ	39	Ⓐ	Ⓑ	Ⓒ	Ⓓ
29	Ⓐ	Ⓑ	Ⓒ	Ⓓ	40	Ⓐ	Ⓑ	Ⓒ	Ⓓ
30	Ⓐ	Ⓑ	Ⓒ	Ⓓ	41	Ⓐ	Ⓑ	Ⓒ	Ⓓ
31	Ⓐ	Ⓑ	Ⓒ	Ⓓ	42	Ⓐ	Ⓑ	Ⓒ	Ⓓ
32	Ⓐ	Ⓑ	Ⓒ	Ⓓ	43	Ⓐ	Ⓑ	Ⓒ	Ⓓ
33	Ⓐ	Ⓑ	Ⓒ	Ⓓ	44	Ⓐ	Ⓑ	Ⓒ	Ⓓ
34	Ⓐ	Ⓑ	Ⓒ	Ⓓ	45	Ⓐ	Ⓑ	Ⓒ	Ⓓ

INQUIRY AND DECISION MAKING									
47	Ⓐ	Ⓑ	Ⓒ	Ⓓ	49	Ⓐ	Ⓑ	Ⓒ	Ⓓ